Th

Economic Question

ECONOMICS TODAY
Edited by Andrew Leake

The *Economics Today* series surveys contemporary headline topics
in applied economics. Each book in the series is written by an expert
in the field in a style that is fluently readable. It serves the student
of introductory economic principles while also making the subject
accessible to a more general reader. The series embraces the
problem-solving skills of the new generation of students and stresses
the importance of real-world issues and the significance of economic
ideas.

Published

Andrew Leake: **The Economic Question**
Jean-Louis Barsoux and Peter Lawrence: **The Challenge of British
    Management**
S. F. Goodman: **The European Community**
Jenny Wales: **Investigating Social Issues**

Forthcoming

Frank Burchill: **Labour Relations**

THE ECONOMIC QUESTION

Andrew Leake

MACMILLAN

First published 1990

Published by
MACMILLAN EDUCATION LTD
Houndmills, Basingstoke, Hampshire RG21 2XS
and London
Companies and representatives
throughout the world

Typeset by Latimer Trend and Company Ltd, Plymouth

Printed in Hong Kong

British Library Cataloguing in Publication Data
Leake, Andrew
The economic question. — (Economics Today series).
1. Economics
I. Title   II. Series
330
ISBN 0–333–53190–6 (hardcover)
ISBN 0–333–53191–4 (paperback)

For Alisoun

Of the roote of this sevene synns, thanne, is Pride, the general roote of alle harmes. For of this roote spryngen certain braunches, as Ire (Wrath), Envye, Accidie or Slewthe (Sloth), Avarice or Coveitise (Covetousness), Glotonye, and Lecherye.

(Chaucer, 'The Parson's Tale', *The Canterbury Tales*, 1340)

Contents

List of Tables and Figures

A Message to the Haves and the Have-nots

1

Compare the economic progress of two economies. One has little in the way of buildings or machinery, has an uneducated population with high birth and death rates, and produces little except by way of subsistence agriculture. In bad years it cannot produce enough food for its own people, and the pressure to survive drives out any concern for the local environment or wildlife. The other country has buildings, machinery and equipment in plenty, and provides its citizens with housing, food, entertainment and all the other features of advanced industrial society. Its concerns are with the quality of life, including the protection of endangered species and threats to the environment, across the globe. Which of these countries is the more successful? What can economics tell us about that success, how it is achieved, and how it reflects the motivation and behaviour of the people involved?

This economic question is the one that dominates our age: what explains the production of goods and services, how each is achieved, and for whom? Why, for instance, can the European community spend money to stop farmers producing food, or to destroy what is seen as overproduction, while people in East Africa face starvation? How can the peoples of the world destroy their environment, cutting down rain forest or throwing away waste that is high in CFCs? Should the allocation of income and wealth between people be determined by central government in the interests of all, or not?

These are all aspects of the central economic question although the details and areas of each enquiry pan out from that centre in all

1

sorts of directions. Essentially, the problems faced by individuals, nations and the world as a whole have these common features. Production depends on the use of resources and those resources are in limited supply. Consumption is desirable in order to satisfy people's wants and those wants, in general, are without limit. Thus it is possible to satisfy some wants but not others. You can have champagne but only by going without something else, and by depriving someone else of the bottle. That is what gives champagne part of its appeal, after all.

But the same sorts of options apply to everything else. At any one time we can consume more in the advanced countries of the world only if they consume less in the developing countries. But this is not always a balanced swap. Advanced countries have research, marketing and packaging industries to create new demands and, through obsolescence, to terminate old ones. This is our contemporary gluttony. It is bad for the glutton who indulges to the point of excess, where consumption yields no satisfaction. It is even worse for other people, however, who are forced to do without by the glutton's excess. The glutton is the dog in the manger who takes for himself what he does not really enjoy, and deprives others of what they very much want. Most of modern consumerism is not at all like this, of course. Consumers are increasingly expert at choosing exactly what to buy with their limited funds to achieve maximum satisfaction. They research the different features and value for money of each product. They complain about poor service. They play their economic part very well.

Yet it is interesting to see how developing countries imitate their rich, trading partners when they start out on the high production, high consumption path. Often the first signs of 'high-level' production are the billboards: open land for miles, a dirt-track road, and towering poster billboards. What do they advertise? – cigarettes perhaps, or cola, or batteries for portable radios. Which aspects of high-spending consumer society do people in developing countries aspire to? Largely that of any aspiring youngsters in the same society, for the vermouth, chocolates and video film world of conspicuous, successful consumerism. If people genuinely want these goods, choose freely to buy them and gain the most satisfaction they can by spending their money this way, then so be it. Economic justice is served. But if the decisions to buy are influenced from outside, imperfectly made and result in consumption that does not offer real satisfaction then there is a problem. And what if people's wants are not reflected equally in offers to buy, because they do not all have the income needed to back up their wants? The only true glutton is a rich one.

Why the Rich Get Richer

The central economic question is one of choice. All economic production is limited at any one time by the resources available to be used. Yet the wants of consumers to be fed, clothed, housed, entertained and pleased in a myriad of other ways: these wants are without limit. Some can be satisfied but only if others are not. Choices have to be made about which consumer wants to satisfy and which not, so that resources can be put to work to make certain products instead of others. Economics is the study of this central fact of life – scarcity – and mankind's response to it. It is a study of decision-making. It is of value, therefore, as training to anyone preparing for a decision-making role in the practical world. Running a household, spending your allowance, managing a business or administering any organisation involves economic decision-making. Choice is the central feature of economic life.

It may seem insulting to compare the choices of affluent, Western consumers for second cars, pets, haute cuisine or whatever with those forced on the poor and the hungry in Third World countries (Table 1.1). In terms of method, approach and technique, however, economists are trained so that they can be dispassionately objective. The essentials of any economic situation are the same and choices always have to be made. They are merely different choices. Both the rich and the poor have resources available to use: they are merely different amounts and types of resources. Both the glutton and the beggar have wants to be satisfied but, again, they are different wants expressed with different economic force because of the spending power available to back them up. What then are the general forms of resources and wants shared by people who appear, in all other respects, to have so little in common?

Economic resources are the basic inputs into the productive process and, in general terms, the same the world over. Every form of production needs at least some of each factor. Land provides a site but also all the minerals, earth and other raw materials located

TABLE 1.1
World Living Standards

Selected countries	Population (millions) mid-1986	GNP per head dollars 1986	Growth ann. av. % 1980–6
Bhutan	1.3	150	unknown
Kenya	21.2	300	3.4
Bolivia	6.6	600	−3.0
Turkey	51.5	1100	4.9
Korea	41.5	2370	8.2
Spain	38.7	4860	1.8
UK	56.7	8870	2.3
Germany	60.9	12 080	1.5
Kuwait	1.8	13 890	−0.9
USA	241.6	17 480	3.1

SOURCE   World Bank, *World Development Report* (New York: Oxford University Press, 1988).

on, under or above that site. Labour provides human effort, both physical and mental. Capital takes the form of money, buildings, machinery and stocks of work in progress. Enterprise is risk capital that employs and organises the work of other factors in anticipation that there will be sales and profit, but at a risk that there may not. Notice with these factors that land on its own is not productive: even hunters and scavengers who 'live off the land' must use their human labour and weapons or tools as well. Notice also how economic production itself determines the amount and type of resources available: education and health care improve labour, experience and training improve enterprise, and factories themselves produce machinery and equipment. So production is needed in order to achieve further production.

That adds to the problem of satisfying wants and making choices between them. Some wants can be satisfied today by using productive resources to make consumption goods. But more wants can be satisfied tomorrow if resources are invested in producing machinery and other capital goods instead. Capital goods give no satisfaction themselves but allow for greater production and satisfaction in future. So one of the choices to be made is between today's wants and tomorrow's: bread today or jam tomorrow. Part of the cycle of poverty comes from using all available resources to stay alive now with none available for investment for the future. The danger point in a subsistence economy is when farmers have to eat their seed corn just to survive, leaving nothing to plant for next year and no way to survive then. Rich countries can afford high investment and even more production in future. Inevitably, therefore, the rich grow richer and the poor grow poorer.

You Have Wants, I Have Needs

We are all consumers and we we all have consumption wants. The wants that are registered in economics are equivalent to those you express in a shop rather than in window shopping: the intention to buy, backed up by purchasing power. To some extent or other everybody wants some of everything that is available. This is the sense in which consumer wants are unlimited. Even if you have enough of one particular good, so that more would make you perhaps literally sick of it, there will be other goods (medicine for a start?) that you will want instead. The wants that are expressed in intentions to buy are strictly limited by income and prices, however, so that consumption choices have already been made.

All wants are relative in economics. Each desire is measured against other desires and that comparison is used as the basis of choice. If only one want was considered as 'the one you just have to get' there would be no consideration between alternatives and no choice about which of infinite wants is the greatest. This would be irrational. Thus there is no place in the world of economics for absolute statements. We all tend, for instance, to consider our own wants to be more important than those of others. We may go so far as to think that others only want something but that we really need it. But there are no 'needs' in economics: there are only relative wants of different strengths.

Affluent consumers who can afford more than enough food, drink, clothing, housing and the other basics of life are familiar with this approach. The relative values of economics are well suited to their situation and consumption decisions that are often finely balanced. But what about when the fine balance is between life and death? Consumption of food and drink, shelter and basic hygiene, is 'necessary' to life. If these wants go unsatisfied due to shortages of resources then starvation, exposure and disease are the result. The problem economists face with this wants-satisfying approach is then exposed: some consumption decisions are irreversible.

If you choose not to eat until you die, you cannot then change your mind, reverse the decision, make up for it some other way. Other decisions may be equally irreversible. If a nuclear power chooses to produce power from unsafe power stations, or to dispose of contaminated waste unsafely, the effects are spread far and wide as from the Chernobyl disaster. Those effects cannot be reversed or cancelled by anyone, after they have happened. If environmental pollution damages the ozone layer that protects the earth from solar radiation that harm cannot be repaired, perhaps for generations to come. Thus some choices may be misguided, based on short-term gain without knowledge of irreversible, long-term damage. Life and death decisions of consumption are especially significant.

Economists are trained in dispassionate and objective analysis, however, and their response can appear insulting to those on the borderline of wants satisfaction. Life-maintaining wants are relative, and comparable to other, life-enhancing wants. There can be no doubt that the level of wants-satisfaction is greater and that resources would be better used to feed the hungry and clothe the poor, were other things equal. But objectivity allows us to recognise that other things are not equal and that the poor do not have the purchasing power to command resources. Their wants, however strong in comparison with others, will carry much less weight in the economic market place, where money speaks for the strength of relative wants.

Where does this dispassionate, objective and damning observation lead us? As economists we are trained in observation, understanding and prediction. Objectively we can explain the causes of poverty and understand why it persists. We can predict how different approaches to it might help. But it is only as civilians, as people with our own values, feelings and humanity, that we can assert what we believe should or should not be done. We must change out of the uniform of professional economics into the mufti of subjective opinion, and realise decisively that we are doing so, to cast our vote as we wish. Most economists use their understanding of the economic world to support a view that development needs guidance and poverty needs assistance, to overcome what are otherwise severe and intransigent problems. Differences arise on the matter of what form and degree of intervention would work best. Let us build on the essentials of economic resources, wants and choices to see how development can improve production, and how different development plans might help.

Production

Finite resources limit the amount that can be made of any product at any one time. Most day to day choices may be concerned with whether to produce more of one good and less of another and how to improve efficiency altogether. It illustrates the range of choice most clearly, however, to concentrate on the border of what can be done at best. Fixed technical conditions limit the amount that could be made, at best, of each good and service. Limited overall resources mean that more of one product can only be made at the expense of having less of another. Production possibilities, therefore, are finite and traded off between alternatives. This is shown for two typical products made by one economy in Figure 1.1.

Notice that this economy can easily produce amounts of each product from within its production possibilities. But to produce within capacity is not best, implies waste of scarce resources and inefficient production decisions. This may be where most economies and most producers actually find themselves, of course, in a land of unemployment, confused management information, with land and equipment to spare. The best outcome is to produce on the frontier of knowledge, at the boundary of what is or is not possible. But this could imply any combination of one good with the other. The more resources are used to make one, the less is left to make the other.

It might be possible to switch easily from one form of industry to the other, or there might even be advantages, called economies of scale, in concentrating more and more resources in one area. This example, however, suggests that it becomes harder and harder to raise production of one good at the expense of its alternative. Unsuitable land, inappropriate machinery and ill-trained labour have to transfer between industries. This is the principle of diminishing returns, so important in much of production economics. It implies that successive increases in production are harder to achieve. The more a poor country tries to produce its own food and to drop

FIGURE 1.1
Production Possibilities

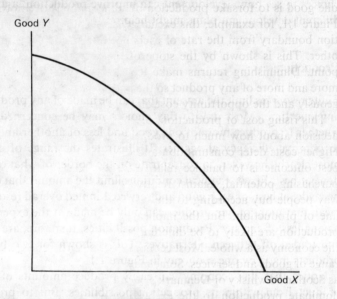

Good *Y*

Good *X*

production of other, longer-term requirements, the harder it may find it to do so.

Counting the Cost

We are all used to counting the cost of our decisions as consumers in terms of the money, the price we have to pay. But as the study of choice economics is rather more exact in its definition of cost, every choice involves a decision between alternatives, and the opportunity cost of that decision, as it is called, is the cost measured in terms of the next best alternative foregone. That may be expressed in money terms, and may be reflected accurately in the price paid, but it does not have to be that way. Thus national decisions about production, investment and development also involve costs, opportunity costs in what must be given up to achieve each.

Production possibilities show the trade-off that is possible between one good and another. This measures the cost of production in true, economic terms. The cost of producing one unit more of one good is to forsake production of some amount of another. In Figure 1.1, for example, this exchange is measured on the production boundary from the rate of exchange out of one good into the other. This is shown by the slope of the production line at each point. Diminishing returns make it increasingly difficult to make more and more of any product so the line changes slope disadvantageously and the opportunity cost of extra production rises.

This rising cost of production, of course, will itself influence the decision about how much to produce and which wants to satisfy. Higher costs deter consumption and lower costs encourage it. The best outcome is to balance relative wants, as expressed through purchasing potential, against relative costs of production. In this way people buy according to the value for money offered by each line of production. But the implications of opportunity costs of production are likely to be different for individual producers from the economy as a whole. Most economies gain from production of a range of goods and services. Some may be national specialities, such as Scotland's whisky or Denmark's bacon, but these are not going to dominate production to the exclusion of all else. Scottish firms produce housing, clothes, bacon and so forth as well. As individual producers, however, they do so by specialising so that no firm produces all these goods but each produces a separate one. Similarly, workers and machines and land specialise in different tasks within their production process.

Specialisation is endemic in society, taken for granted these days and built into class, housing, social attitudes and so much else. We categorise people according to their specialist training, work or experience. We identify areas, such as parkland, coastline or shopping centre by its localised function. And opportunity cost again measures all these differences. Where labour is plentiful and relatively unskilled, agriculture is labour intensive to reflect the low opportunity cost of workers. The same crops may be produced elsewhere using tractors and mechanisation to reflect these resources low, local cost. Workers attend to different tasks in the process of production, on a building site or a car assembly plant, for example, to improve efficiency from division of labour.

Specialists gain experience, learn by doing, and contribute at lower opportunity cost to the production of each good or service. But specialists produce different things, obviously, so specialisation requires exchange before its gains can be realised. The process of specialisation and exchange is at the heart of economic society, and of immense significance not only for the efficient us of each nation's resources. It leads also to the path of development through trade.

Finding Room to Grow

How is an economy to achieve the growth it needs to become better off? It can raise production of just one good, such as food, but only at the expense of others such as investment goods, roads or drainage. It can overcome inefficiency and take fuller account of existing technology to reach its potential in terms of production possibilities. But long-term growth requires an expansion of that potential, to move the frontier line of possibilities outwards. This is the route to economic development. The scientists and technicians of the country play an essential part here in advancing the level of knowledge and practical application that sets the technical conditions governing production. But the economics of production suggest that the main issue has to be the level of factor inputs that can be used. More factors allow more output and rising living standards.

How is the frontier of production possibilities to be shifted outwards? Land and its natural resources is a vital factor of production and one that a country may be able to find more of by reclamation. This raises important and wider questions, however. In Africa and elsewhere there is pressure on natural species – zebra, rhino, elephant, the large cats, and many more – that has led to the extinction of some and a threat to many more. This threat comes partly from hunting, or poaching for tusks, horns or skins. Mainly it comes from the local people's acquisition of land. What has traditionally been wilderness, a natural habitat for wildlife, is unproductive in the economic sense for all except a few hunters and their successors in tourism. A growing population, a growing economy requires more land to build on, and to farm, and to use for timber and minerals. We have already reached the stage in most developing countries where wildlife and wilderness must be justified on specific grounds, be they economic, commercial or for national values, in order to protect and preserve that environment. Without official and active protection, they go.

Official national policy has no place for Western, animal-loving sentiment. Land is a major resource and wildlife is seen, as local tribes have always seen it, as a commercial opportunity. But there are some countries where this opportunity claims a lower priority than others in mining, farming or manufacturing. Official government policy is often in favour of land development. The decimation of the Amazonian rain forest is a source of economic growth to the countries involved, and a lucrative business for the individuals concerned. It yields top quality hardwoods for export and converts 'waste' land into a productive factor input. The world environment may suffer if this continues, from an accelerating greenhouse effect due to reduced consumption of carbon dioxide by world plant life, but poorer countries' development will be damaged if they stop. As they see it, why should they not continue in their country the process already completed in England, France and other developed nations?

Not many countries are so fortunate as the UK in being able to reclaim land, in the sense of an economic resource, literally from under the sea. North Sea oil resources became available through improved technology, at a cost warranted by the continuing value of oil. How fortunate it was to enjoy this new source of raw materials in a true environmental wasteland, out of sight and out of mind for most of the people, most of the time. How encouraging if further economic development could be based on sea-bed exploitation – even better out in space. But the sight of oil rigs on the beaches and beauty spots of the south coast brings the development issue much closer to home, and generally the developers win. Which raises perhaps one other route to land development, and one that has scarred Europe more deeply than any environmental damage yet. The drive to acquire land, its resources and its productive wealth has always been one of the motives for waging war. If land cannot be reclaimed, or discovered, or developed it may still be stolen from others, to the economic benefit of the (victorious) citizens.

Investing in the Future

Existing land can be improved in terms of productive potential, as with the North Sea and the Amazon rain forest. People's labour can be improved by adding to their skills, experience, abilities and attitudes in general. The key to all this, as with so much else in economic development however, lies in capital investment. Investment is the main source of growth. It adds to the stock of capital equipment, buildings, machinery and so forth. It can take the form of research and technical development to stretch the boundaries of productive know-how. It can raise the yield of land and educate labour for high-level productivity. And in all this the factor input of capital is itself man-made, and, given the productive resources, can be expanded infinitely. The country that invests successfully grows fast and develops fully allowing, in turn, more investment and more growth. The country that cannot afford to invest does not grow at all.

Clearly it is the level of investment that matters but also the nature and quality of that investment (Table 1.2). Investment is spending on new capital stock, as buildings, equipment and stocks. Some of this is needed year by year on a regular basis just to replace old equipment as it wears out from productive use. This is called depreciation. Other investment will be to acquire additional machines of the old type, or new equipment of improved technical specification. All this is influenced by the cost of funds borrowed for investment, which is the rate of interest on loans, and the expected rate of return on new projects. But there may be wider development issues as well.

Government may wish to direct investment into community projects to develop the infrastructure of the national economy, and so provide roads, communications, power, education and health. This may be justified more in terms of general benefits to the society and the development of the economy than on strictly commercial grounds. But political judgements might steer public investment in a different direction, into armaments, public buildings and high prestige, high-profile developments. Free enterprise takes account only of commercial returns, but this can give short-term profitability the priority over long-term national interest. The balance can be a difficult one.

An advanced industrial economy has the wealth creation power to finance its own investment for the future, although clearly some countries are much more successful than others in this. Many less developed nations are too poor, and too concerned with the pressing priority to offer basic consumption to their citizens, to achieve the

TABLE 1.2
How Much Investment?

Country	Net Investment (as % of GDP)	Growth (av. ann. % change, GDP per head)
Ghana	6.4	−1.7
Bolivia	8.8	1.3
Argentina	14.0	1.3
Group of 10 developing economies with low growth	10.8	0.4
Turkey	13.8	3.1
Brazil	19.3	4.4
Hong Kong	26.6	6.1
Group of 14 developing economies with high growth	18.4	4.5

SOURCE World Bank, *World Development Report* (New York: Oxford University Press, 1986).

same levels of saving and investment. Some can hardly invest at all. The path to development would be completely blocked, therefore, were it not for investment from abroad. They must borrow from governments, companies and individuals in other countries in order to maintain their development process. At best, the opportunities for commercial return in a relatively undeveloped economy will be great, and the speed of the development process will allow a quick repayment of the loans. In practice, however, many Third World countries have seen their rescuers become gaolers and their palaces of investment become prisons of debt repayment.

Snakes and Ladders

The Third World debt problem is of such a scale that it threatens not only the future of the developing nations but also the banking system of the developing world. The loans involved are colossal. They were justified at the start by the lower interest rates on borrowing and the high return from these countries' exports of primary products – coffee, timber, sugar, copper, etc. World prices changed, world interest rates changed, and debtor nations found that their foreign earnings were barely enough to pay interest charges, let alone repay capital, and nowhere near buying much-needed capital equipment. The cycle of debt was that experienced by any individual in the same, sorry position, with one difference. International banks had lent so much, and faced the threat of receiving so little of it back in interest or capital repayment, that a banking collapse seemed, for a time, a strong possibility. Now many debts have been rescheduled, and further changes in interest rates and primary product prices could remove the crisis altogether. And the governments of the advanced industrial nations have played a part also.

Poor countries seeking sponsors to set them on the path to investment and development often turn to the governments of the rich nations. Some of these have strong political motives to help out. They lend generously, perhaps as aid at low interest rates, or as a gift. But there can be strings. They may require political support, as with 'satellite' nations tied economically to the USA or the USSR. They may direct the path of development to supply resources to their own industries, or to buy capital goods from their own producers. The game of development is played on a board with snakes of crippling debt going down and ladders of investment opportunity going up. Links with world powers and other major countries may lead in either direction.

Such economic links have a long, long pedigree. Until quite recently, the perks of empire allowed a rich nation to invest relatively little – a few convicts, some livestock, fruit trees, a fort or two perhaps – in order to extract what it wished in the way of natural resources and primary products. Now the independence of nation states, for the most part, allows countries to sell their products at realistic prices. Still, however, the process of development is intrinsically linked with international trade.

Free trade offers all the advantages of free enterprise whereby individual motivation promotes opportunities for profit through producing what consumers wish to buy, in order to satisfy as many wants as possible. Trade takes this further by extending the advantages of specialisation and exchange to the factors of production in different countries, for their mutual benefit. This is shown for advanced, industrial nations in the achievements of the European Community. When the six original members formed the Community the UK stayed out. Since then the growth of those countries has been remarkable, around twice that of the UK, and enough to encourage the UK and five other nations to join.

The EC is a political and social community with specific economic policies besides, but its essential feature is a customs union. With the completion of the Single European Market in 1992 this should offer the largest free trade area in the world with no internal barriers to exchange of products or resources, and a common external tariff, or import tax, on imports from outside. This market is so large, prosperous and open that any firm, in any one member country, can set up shop and specialise in selling one product to millions of consumers. Consumers can choose freely from a limitless range of products and producers. Thus trade offers choice and opportunity, but also it offers growth and improved living standards. What is so significant to the developing countries of the world, however, is the way basic economic principles show that trade benefits are available to both richer and poorer partners in the exchange.

Specialisation and Exchange

What are the gains from trade? Compare two countries that each produce different goods. Clearly, trade is valuable here to allow consumers a choice. Exchange is beneficial to both and all that is in question is how much of one good will be exchanged for the other. The appeal of empire was in laying down terms for this exchange, or the terms of trade as it is called, entirely in the powerful country's favour. Trade in the EC is more balanced but continues along these traditional lines in exchanging one country's brands, models and national products for another: perhaps real English tea for Belgium paté, or Fiat cars for Jaguars. But most products can be made these days in any country at all. Trade still makes sense to exchange the products that one country makes best for what another country makes best. Economic theory goes one step better, however, to explain trade between unequal partners.

The theory of comparative advantage explains trade between two partners, be they countries or individuals in the same society, that is based on nothing but a difference in production cost (Figure 1.2).

FIGURE 1.2
Specialisation and Trade

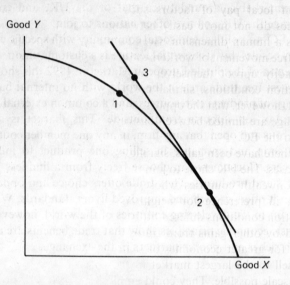

1. Self-sufficient countries are limited by their own production possibilities.
2. Specialisation allows them to take advantage of their comparative advantage in production.
3. Trade with other countries brings benefits: consumption beyond what they can produce for themselves.

One country, such as Germany, may be more efficient than Britain at producing both goods. But if Britain has a relative advantage, or more exactly less of a disadvantage at one of the goods than at the other, there is a case for specialisation and exchange. Britain will specialise in whatever she does at least disadvantage in order that Germany can specialise in whatever she does best.

Specialisation, therefore, is at the heart of international trade, cooperation and exchange. But it is at the heart of economic society in general, and the reason is the same: specialisation allows the best use of different production possibilities. Now those possibilities might become quite similar if countries exchange know-how or resources to overcome production disadvantages. Market forces encourage this to happen by reflecting relative scarcity in the different local pay of factors such as labour and capital. But resources do not move easily between countries, especially where there is a human dimension. Even in the single European Market where free movement of workers to jobs is now permitted, people do not readily uproot themselves from family and friends. Similar production conditions, similar costs and similar factor prices do suggest, however, that the opportunities for gains from comparative advantage are limited between basically similar economies such as those in the EC.

Yet there have been gains, significant gains from trade in this and other cases. The UK chose to join the EC, forsaking trade links with Commonwealth countries whose production possibilities differed greatly, in preference for neighbouring trading partners whose production conditions differed little. The apparent self-sacrifice was justified by other gains from trade, and mainly the opportunities offered for greater economies of scale in production. British firms could sell to the largest market in the world and produce on the largest scale possible. They could employ the most efficient, indivisible equipment, the best specialists, the best techniques, and so cut unit costs of production. It takes merger, reorganisation and investment to respond to this opportunity, and those who do not, face tougher competition from abroad. But the winners cut costs, improve quality, stimulate further growth and maintain the dynamic development of the economy. A prize worth the effort.

Which Way Forward?

There is much that the advanced, industrial world has shown the developing world about growth and rising living standards. With the benefit of hindsight they might claim that some of it was good and some bad. Investment is needed to accumulate more resources for production, and trade is needed to gain the benefits of specialisation. Broadly there appear to be three main paths that a less developed country might choose to follow. One is the free market path of enterprise, competition and trade. Another is one of collective control, ownership and direction. The last is to forsake altogether the goal of a consumption oriented, industrialised economy. Which of these paths might modern economics be said to light most clearly?

Free market economics is the basis of the subject as we study it here, and on all conventional, introductory courses in the West. Scarcity and choice prompt individual decisions motivated by individual return in the form of satisfaction, income and profit. Specialisation allows the best possible use of scarce resources but requires exchange through free markets, where relative price determines the quantity and allocation of resources and products. At an international level this exchange is again arranged freely through forces of supply and demand to reflect relative scarcity and to make best use of resources, in line with the principle of comparative advantage.

Countries that choose to follow this path must allow free enterprise to blossom and prices and pay to reflect market pressures. The distribution between rich and poor may become wider, indeed it may need to if the wealth-creating sector is to accumulate substantial savings for their investment and growth. This is the route chosen by South Korea, Macao, Singapore, Taiwan and other newly industrialising countries, with such success. Their growth has been remarkable and seems likely to place them as rivals to Japan in industrial power by the turn of the century. It is little wonder that many other countries seek to follow suit.

Socialist countries distrust the capitalist direction of this form of development. They plan their growth systematically, with priority given to investment in basic areas such as heavy industry and infrastructure rather than consumer convenience. They determine the ownership, employment and return to resources centrally in terms of the overall development plan. But this can be inflexible, and the individual motivation that is called profit in free enterprise may emerge as corruption instead.

Both approaches share the central economic concern to make maximum use of scarce resources, if by very different methods. They share also a determination to move as quickly as possible along the growth path of industrial development. What is much rarer is for a country's people to turn away from material acquisition altogether. Bhutan is high in the Himalayas, physically and culturally remote from the rest of the world. On most economic scales it is the poorest nation on earth, and a ripe target for the free enterprise and communist forces on each side. But 97 per cent of Bhutan's people are subsistence farmers and Buddhists who see work as a fulfilment and life as a simple, religious experience. Their head of state is an absolute monarch who sees the interests of his people served best by protection from the sophisticated, material world. There is no hunger, unemployment, begging, crime or overpopulation. The people live much as they have always done. Their country would be called undeveloped, but are they less content than we? Perhaps they ask questions for which economics does not hold the answers.

Was the Garden of Eden Ever Really 'Green'?

The race to economic development attracts some single-minded competitors. The drive is to make full productive use of existing resources and to develop new ones. This leaves little room for concern about the environment and a low priority for measures to protect it. Scarcity value applies to green issues as with everything else: the countries that have developed furthest have least left in terms of natural, unspoiled habitat. It is the most advanced countries, typically, who are the most vociferous in championing green policies. Most greens are city dwellers. But less developed countries have much more wilderness land to spare, and a familiarity with wildlife that can breed contempt. Why should they share the fashion for environmentalism unless it is made relevant to them in terms of tourism, production costs or supporting investment? Environmentalism might be seen with health or fitness, after all, as an advanced form of consumer affluence.

How can the two patterns of consumption coexist? Affluent consumerism encourages the packaging, dispensers, conspicuous expense and designer obsolescence that distinguish our modern form of gluttony. We may not eat too much, but our way of life uses many resources when a few would do and invents new wants that we did not know we felt. At the same time, we turn to dieting and fitness products, official food surpluses and Third World aid. Are these ensuring the satisfaction of wants at lowest opportunity cost, as the central economic question would require? The innocent consumer in an undeveloped Garden of Eden was spared all these choices. But perhaps it is only through deliberate choice that we can show true concern for the environment anyway.

Work for the Workers 2

In the words of Voltaire 'work banishes those three great evils, boredom, vice, and poverty'. But there have always been unemployed people without work who have provoked different, and often opposed, reactions. Some people, and not necessarily the hardest working, assume that the unemployed have chosen to be out of work in some way: that they are shirkers, preferring a life of boredom, vice and poverty. Others are more compassionate and blame the circumstances rather than the individual. To them the unemployed are people to whom no work is offered but who are essentially, potentially still workers. Those that Franklin D. Roosevelt called 'the forgotten men at the bottom of the economic pyramid'. So how do economists ally themselves with these positions? Do they see the unemployed as lazy shirkers or wasted workers?

The issue divides economists and economics rather as it divides others. There are different types of unemployment, different causes of the problem and different solutions suggested to remove it. This issue may become more or less significant from time to time, but it has absorbed economists almost constantly in the advanced, industrial age. In the 1930s, the world slump became the dominant issue of the day and its images of dole queues, baffled government ministers and New Deal policies remain with us still. The Jarrow marchers of the 1930s were followed by their successors in unemployment two generations later; the numbers unemployed in the UK were higher at times in the 1980s than in the 1930s. Unemployment shot up between 1979 and 1982 from 5 per cent to 12 per cent, and then stayed at around that level for much of the 1980s.

Unemployment makes the headlines not just when it is high or rising, however; it can improve and be a source of good news as well (Table 2.1). In 1988 and 1989, the total of registered unemployed fell suddenly and substantially. The government could claim that its policies were working and that it had found the solution to the underlying problems of the British economy. This would imply, of course, that registered unemployment is in some sense a symptom of the general state of the economy. How might that be so?

TABLE 2.1
UK Unemployment

	Workforce in employment (million)	*Unemployment (adult) (million)*
1982	23.3	2.63
1983	23.1	2.87
1984	23.5	3.00
1985	24.61	3.04
1986	24.74	3.11
1987	24.37	2.82
1988	26.20	2.30

SOURCE   *Economic Progress Report* (London: HM Treasury, 1989).

Labour is a vital resource. The sweat from one's brow or the power of the mind must be channelled to produce any goods and services. In an advanced economy such as the British there is a huge stock of capital equipment for that labour to work with, but even so payments to labour claim most of the national income. In developing economies, as we saw in the last chapter, labour and land may have to be responsible for much more of production on their own. Whatever the significance of labour relative to other factors, to use anything less than all that is available is clearly to waste economic resources. In turn, this implies producing less in the economy than could possibly be produced and satisfying fewer wants as a result.

Unemployment, therefore, signifies waste and inefficiency and that the economic system has broken down in some way.

It is generally recognised also that unemployment is a serious concern in its own right. Unemployment occurs when people are without work and looking for work but unable to find it. This definition excludes those who are occupied in ways other than full time unemployment: full-time students, full-time house-parents, or knights of the road. It implies directly, however, that unemployed people are being prevented and denied work and the satisfaction of their wants for some reason or other. In practice they are likely to suffer in a social as well as an economic sense, for the work ethic still runs deep and strong through British society. Those out of work may feel a loss of purpose and a loss of identity, except of course as the group to which they have already been allocated so disparagingly here – 'the unemployed'.

Who Are the Unemployed?

Two million is a great number of people. It would be difficult to identify such a number as having anything much in common, but that is what economists do in trying to describe, analyse and explain unemployment. But things are more complicated still in that the aggregate consists of a shifting mass, many of whom just pass through. In a given hour there may be 100 000 people, say, both in Wembley Stadium and in Victoria station, but those at Wembley stay watching there all that time and do not leave while those at the station pass briefly in and out on their way to somewhere else. The unemployment total includes both types: the long-term residents and short-term visitors.

Transitional unemployment occurs when people move out of one job and into another, but not straight away. At lower levels of pay especially and in casual, unskilled jobs this may be a very common pattern. Thus frictional unemployment is normal and a sign that the job market is operating positively to create new posts and to attract workers into them. Changing the rules for registration of the jobless to include only those without work after a few weeks will remove this casual unemployment from the figures.

Other unemployment is much more worrying because it affects workers for months or even years at a time. This is a symptom of breakdown in the job market and a cause of persistent hardship. The longer one stays out of work, the more difficult it is to persuade employers of one's ability, and the harder it is to respond positively to any offers they make. This long-term unemployment may arise in different ways, although there is much argument between economists over how to draw the line between them.

Structural unemployment arises because the people looking for work do not suit, in some sense, the jobs that are available to them. They may be in different areas of the country and unable to transfer accommodation, or require different skills that are difficult to learn. Thus a mismatch occurs between jobs and workers but, as a message of hope, there are at least jobs waiting to be filled if only the workers can adapt to them.

Cyclical unemployment more often occurs because of problems affecting all lines of employment and all types of workers together in the downswing of the national trade cycle. There are not enough jobs on offer in total, never mind of what type or in which area, to employ all the people looking for work. Economists fall into broadly two lines of thought on this: some look mainly at the provision of jobs and show that the need is for higher spending and higher production to create more work for the workers; others look at the faults in the labour market (such as trade unions or government taxes and benefits) that prevent workers from bidding for more work through reduced wage rates.

These two opposing lines of thought are drawn up behind the Keynesian and New Classicist banners respectively, and identified with rather different views of the unemployed themselves. Each side tends to parody its opponents, of course, but the distinction might be expressed thus: are the unemployed merely poor, hapless victims of an inefficient, entrepreneurial economy, or are they shirkers without initiative who have chosen voluntary unemployment in preference to hard, if lower paid work?

A Market for Labour

Our view of people out of work must depend on our view of work itself. In economics this is described in terms of the market for labour. We see work as an economic transaction like toothpaste or ice cream, with sellers offering to work and buyers seeking to employ workers. The commodity they exchange is the economic work, both physical and mental, done by labour. Labour is a factor of production wanted by buyers and provided by sellers. It just so happens in this case that the buyers in question are firms who employ workers to make their products. The sellers of labour are the workers themselves. These buyers and sellers are brought together in a market to arrange their exchange.

Some markets in the economy are easily identified by their physical location and organisational arrangements. Insurance underwriters concentrate together in Lloyds of London; fresh fruit and vegetables are traded in wholesale markets. But most markets are much more scattered and diverse than this. Some bring buyers and sellers together only fleetingly on phone lines or by post, across counties or countries. Complicated and scattered markets may consist of many different types of buying and selling that is specialised because of differences in the type of commodity being exchanged. Clearly the labour market is one of these.

Labour can be classified by ability and location. Two identical sisters may have studied different subjects to different levels of education. They may have gained different experience from their previous jobs. All this may be called their human capital, invested to develop their labour. They may simply have natural skills, interests and personalities that separate them. For all these reasons it is unreasonable to place both sisters in the same market for labour: the productive ability that each can offer to the same employer is clearly different. Instead we must consider subdivisions of the labour market drawn to distinguish major types of abilities, such as skilled or unskilled, technical or administrative, and general or professional. These subdivisions become even more significant when we consider location as well. One sister living in the family council house or owner-occupied house in the North-East is unlikely to be able to join the labour market facing her sister in the South-East.

What Jobs on Offer?

The jobs on offer in the labour market at any one time are likely to be similarly diverse. Some require skill, some do not, some are in the North and others in the South. Taken altogether the total demand for workers is measured by those jobs filled by employees and those still left unfilled but advertised as job vacancies. Advertised job vacancies are a measure, therefore, of the spare demand for labour that unemployed workers might satisfy. The official figures of vacancies are like those for unemployment, however, in that they deserve careful interpretation. They also represent a floating population as posts are filled and replaced by new openings. And the official count is of advertisements placed only at government job centres. Many more jobs are offered privately instead through the press, employment agencies or merely on the grapevine.

Job vacancies show the spare demand for labour at any given time. The figure presents this as a fixed value, but of course things might have been very different. Different circumstances would have produced more or less job vacancies, and changed circumstances from time to time do exactly that. But what circumstances matter most? This is a question that the trained economist responds to immediately. Economists analyse systematically, looking for a common pattern in apparently disjointed events. They also analyse theoretically, starting with general predictions that are most likely to be relevant. Here the target is the demand for labour, and top of the list of likely influences stands a common culprit: the level of wages.

Workers' wages are their cost of employment, their price in the labour market. Subdivisions in the market bring differences in prices so that some people earn high wages while others earn less. In general, wages are significant in setting the number of jobs on offer and the number of registered job vacancies. To see how, we must put ourselves in the position of an employer, paying wages to employ workers in production. How are we likely to respond to a rise in wages? Clearly, this will mean that each worker costs us more money, but for no corresponding change in output or value to the firm. Some workers, and maybe all, will now cost us more than they are worth. As a company we would have to stop employing those workers. We cut our job offers, our advertised vacancies, and our demand for labour. Conversely, a fall in wage costs allows us to profit by increasing the number of vacancies in order to raise employment.

These changes to the demand for labour are shown in terms of Figure 2.1. The demand curve for labour, as it is known, shows all the levels of employment that firms would seek to achieve at each possible wage. To draw this we must assume that all other influences on demand, for the time being at least, remain constant. At any one

FIGURE 2.1
The Demand for Labour

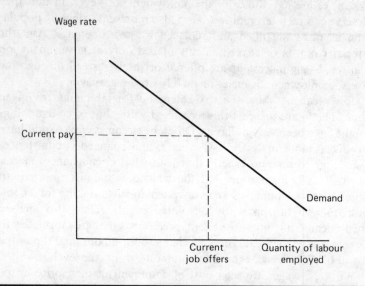

time we can have only one, actual level of wages, and the given figure for job vacancies that this would imply. But a fall in wages, for instance, would cause a movement along the demand curve for labour and a rise in the number of jobs on offer. But would this be enough to bring all the unemployed into work, you may ask, and is it really likely to happen? Are wage cuts leading to job creation, the solution to unemployment?

Labour Market Failures

Wage cuts should create jobs. There is another way also in which they help to remove unemployment. Wages reward work and encourage people to offer their labour to employers. Thus a cut in wages discourages workers and reduces the overall amount of labour that workers wish to offer. We call this a fall in the supply of labour. Discouraged workers do not remain unemployed since they stop looking for work altogether and choose instead to study, say, or stay at home. Others may stay in employment but choose to work fewer hours. This can be illustrated in terms of a move along a supply curve showing workers' offers of labour at each possible pay level, other things being equal (see Figure 2.2).

FIGURE 2.2
Unemployment and Wages

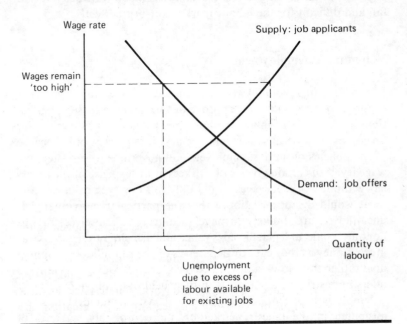

Thus a fall in wages should create jobs and discourage workers, so raising demand and cutting supply. If these market forces work perfectly there can be no unemployment once demand and supply have been matched at the appropriate level of wages. Unemployment can only persist if wages jam at the 'wrong' level for some reason. This is shown in Figure 2.2. But what could cause this to happen? What stops wages falling to remove unemployment?

Unions are in the business of keeping wages up. They try to do so by restricting the supply of workers to their area through a closed shop, perhaps, or by agreeing binding, collective agreements with employers. Governments also aim to regulate and influence labour markets. Minimum wage regulations protect poorly paid workers in employment by keeping their wages up. Benefits such as housing and supplementary benefit protect against poverty but ensure that some low paid workers have a guaranteed income greater than they could earn in employment. Tax rates at low levels of earning may have the same effect and force wages up to compensate for reduced take home pay. Any or all of these influences make it difficult for wage levels to fall and difficult for the labour market to work perfectly.

Voluntary Unemployment

Economists in favour of the free market for the way it matches supply and demand do not approve of this, and see these imperfections as the cause of much unemployment. They call this voluntary unemployment because it is unnecessary. It is present only because of the policies of unions, employers and government to protect the wage levels of certain groups of workers at the expense of the others left without work. If wages would only fall this type of unemployment would disappear. Notice that the particular individuals left unemployed are unlikely to have volunteered themselves for this honour. Some are persuaded by tax and benefit rates to raise as much money as they can for themselves or their families by claiming dole rather than low paid work. Others are left facing too few job offers by restrictive agreements in their field of employment.

Supply is kept from finding its match with demand. There is a mismatch in the labour market or, more probably, a series of mismatches between the different subdivisions of the market. A shortage in one area, perhaps of skilled work or in a locality of high housing costs, persists because wages are stopped from rising. Meanwhile, unemployment exists in areas of unskilled, low paid work. If only wages were more flexible and workers could be matched to the jobs being created the problem might be solved. So what can be done to overcome mismatches?

Conservative governments in the 1980s embraced the market economists' approach to unemployment. The role of government, they said, was to help the market do its work by removing unnecessary imperfections. So they cut the influence of unions over individual workers, through closed shops and secondary industrial action that goes beyond the employer immediately in dispute. They limited access, somewhat, to benefits, and the level of income that benefits could offer relative to paid work. They cut direct tax rates in a number of ways including, through National Insurance contributions and others, the impact of taxation on those starting work at low levels of pay. They cut down on minimum wage protection.

All these policies were intended to end mismatches in the labour market by changing the supply of labour; they were 'supply-side' policies. Workers who were previously on the dole because it paid them, in some sense, to prefer this option to work were being encouraged to offer themselves for employment at lower levels of pay. The greater and more flexible supply of labour should fill available jobs and end voluntary unemployment. But the government also acted to improve demand, through policies of job creation. Partly this was through wage cuts, at low levels of pay especially. Thus the 1980s saw a remarkable increase in the number of part-time and casual workers such as working mothers, students and pensioners, who chose to work rather than not to work, often for low pay, and often instead of full-time, higher paid employees.

Job creation programmes have caught the public eye more commonly from a different perspective, however. Attention has been focused on retraining and vocational preparation through schemes such as the Youth Training Scheme. Major companies have sponsored individuals for education packages 'to train the workers without jobs for the jobs without workers'. Long-term unemployed have been interviewed and guided into individual courses of training. In these and other ways the government could claim the initiative for positive, active job creation. In retrospect, however, it seems likely that the main impact of all this was on public attitudes and expectations rather than the creation of a substantial number of new jobs. Not many of those engaged in YTS ended with a job, unless by replacing other, older, higher paid employees. Not many of the long-term unemployed in the North-East could retrain for new skills or move to new jobs, whatever their initiative or effort in self-education.

But we could see that the government was acting, and we could expect the unemployed to take steps to prepare for work. The expectation was reinforced, and perhaps established in some youngsters, that unemployed people were shirkers who could become workers like everyone else if only they would retrain, or 'get on their bikes', or try for the new jobs being made available. Those directly involved in YTS, worker's education and job placement never really shared this view. But the government could show as proof, by the end of the 1980s, a substantial rise in the number of new jobs that the British economy had created. Employment rose, unemployment fell. Why else could this have happened, but for the success of the government's package of supply-side and job creation policies?

The Battle against Inflation

Our view of unemployment so far has focused upon the position of the individual. Individual workers choose not to work or can find no work to do at current wage rates. Thus it is the sum of individual problems and decisions that makes up the overall level of unemployment. But much of economics takes a broader view than this of the problems and behaviour of the national economy, as if the performance of the whole is explained by more than just the sum of individual parts. This collective, general analysis of the economy and its national aggregates such as growth, inflation and unemployment, is called macroeconomics. We will consider it more fully in Chapters 6 and 7, on inflation and the Budget, later in this book. But in terms of unemployment it is also important to consider macroeconomic issues: the general level of unemployment is affected by general forces in the economy.

The decade of the 1980s brought changing fortunes for the unemployed. In 1981 and 1982, the total number of registered unemployed rose to record levels, but by 1989 job creation had recovered and unemployment fell quickly once more. Macroeconomics leads us to relate this to other forces in the national economy and, for its dominant role in government policy-making if nothing else, we must among these include the battle against inflation. In the early 1980s, inflation was public enemy number one, and the hard won success to reduce inflation coincided with rising unemployment. By the end of the decade the position was reversed and as inflation rose again to worrying levels, the level of unemployment fell.

The significance and duration of this apparent connection between inflation and unemployment is one of the most interesting, but contentious, in macroeconomics. We will return to it more fully when we question the causes and cures of inflation in Chapter 6. But even the monetarist economists who devised government policy in the 1980s would probably accept that some connection exists. At least for a time the weapons used to combat inflation bounce off that target, spin in another direction, and inadvertently harm an innocent bystander. The wounds to the economy are those of 'disinflationary' unemployment.

Disinflationary unemployment happens because the government restricts the growth of the money supply that people have available to spend on goods and services. Reduced spending growth hits firms who cannot afford to pay more to their workers. In a perfect world, perhaps, this would be recognised immediately and exactly by managers and employees alike. Product prices would stop rising, wages would stop rising and inflation would be controlled. But the world is far from perfect, even in this economic sense, so some prices and some wages continue to rise through inflation, at least for a time. And for that time, firms cannot afford to produce so much or employ so many workers. Thus unemployment rises as a cost of inflation failing to fall fast enough. It may be unnecessary, and it may be temporary. But it is likely to be widespread, affecting workers in all types of jobs and all parts of the country, and it may be quite severe.

The Keynesian View

Keynesian economists put much more weight on macroeconomic forces in explaining the general performance of the economy than just this single, and temporary, instance of disinflation. Keynes's own general theory was developed in response to the widespread and intractable problems of the 1930s, but his followers made up the majority of orthodox analysts and policy advisers in the post-war period. The 1970s' inflation pushed some of these ideas out of fashion for a time but the Keynesian alternative is still presented by the opposition, and to a large extent within official government circles as well. This is not the time to cover all those ideas, but their significance for unemployment and its cure is particularly relevant here, to the job creation successes of the late 1980s. Could these show Keynesians making a comeback?

A good starting point is in the connection between jobs and

output. Clearly, firms employ workers to produce output and, other things being equal, firms raise employment in order to increase their output. In macroeconomic terms, therefore, the key to employment (and hence unemployment) lies in the general level of economic activity. Keynesians believe that this can be influenced by the government through the use of what are now orthodox measures such as interest rates, tax levels, and the government's Budget balance. If the government stimulates or reflates the economy by raising spending, even in an artificial way such as borrowing to finance public investments in roads or hospitals, this sets the ball rolling. Extra spending leads to extra production, extra jobs, and lower unemployment. This is also a job creation policy, but it is instigated by the government directly and takes effect generally throughout the national economy rather than with particular individuals.

So how is it possible to tell if job creation and falling unemployment comes as a result of labour market, wage reform, supply-side policies or, alternatively, from Keynesian reflation? We could believe what the government tells us they are doing, or what they think they are doing; but that really is notoriously unreliable. We could observe whether the improvement is coming to pockets of long-term unemployment and employees in certain trades or at certain levels of pay only; but any improvement is likely to spill over quickly to more successful areas anyway and so generate more general, macroeconomic effects.

Perhaps the best clue is, again, in the connection with inflation. Improvements to the structure and performance of the labour market should create jobs and cut wages. There should be no pressure on prices and wages to rise; there should be no problem of inflation. Keynesian reflation is likely to be quite different. This depends on the state of the economy when the government starts to increase national spending, of course, for bottle-necks in certain lines of production or for certain labour skills may come sooner or later. It depends also on how the reflation is managed – through credit creation, say, or public investments. There is likely to come a point, however, when increased spending pressures firms to raise their prices and workers to raise their wages, rather than output and jobs. Inflation then accompanies the job creation, or perhaps even replaces it.

Critics of Keynesian economics believe that this flaws the whole approach. Reflation can create only bogus jobs, only temporarily, they say. Prolonged government action along these lines causes permanent damage when inflation takes over, damaging competitiveness, investment and growth. Thus the only responsible course is to win the battle against inflation first, then create permanent jobs through supply-side reforms to the labour market. This is what we were told by the governments of the 1980s, for example. It is curious, therefore, that the rapid fall in unemployment at the end of the decade was accompanied by the rising inflation which, we have seen, is more a symptom of Keynesian reflation. The long-term success of supply-side job creation policies has yet to be proved.

What's a Fair Wage?

We have considered the level of wages so far only in a general sense, whereby a wage cut discourages some potential workers and encourages job creation to match supply and demand and cure unemployment. Most people would not favour this approach, however, if it only solved the unemployment of some by reducing the wages of all. The hidden feature lies in the nature of that wage level and its significance in the labour market. There are, in fact, many different subdivisions of the market each with their own supply and demand conditions and their own level of wages. Wages are much higher in some parts of the market than in others. Thus wage cuts cure unemployment by creating jobs mainly for the low paid, on the margin of the market. Other groups' wages need not be affected, they hope.

These separate wage levels can be very different indeed. At the foot of the pyramid are the unskilled workers earning a pound or two an hour. At the top sits the investment consultant who charges $2500 for an hour of his time, and the board chairman earning $51 million as one year's salary. Such differences lie at the heart of our society. Doctors and architects are held in respect for the nature of their professional work but also for the rates of pay that such work commands. Chargehands and supervisors expect and are expected to be paid more than those for whom they have responsibility. And yet people's knowledge of others' pay is extremely limited. Most people prefer to keep their own incomes relatively private. Very few workers could say if they were placed in the top, middle or bottom

10 per cent of pay scales in the country, for instance (Table 2.2). Very few could say how much more the top 10 per cent actually get paid than the bottom 10 per cent.

Some of these questions are answered in Table 2.2. On average those in the top fifth of incomes (before taxes and benefits) earn 200 times as much as those in the bottom fifth. But these averages disguise much greater variations, of course. There are some at the very top who earn much more still. There are some at the very bottom who earn nothing at all. These variations are reduced by government taxation and benefits where these follow the Robin Hood principle of helping the poor. But by any standards the differences are still remarkable. Is this fair?

TABLE 2.2
Pay Differences in the UK

Income group	Original household income, on average £	Final income after taxes and benefits £
Bottom fifth	110	3820
Next fifth	2480	4600
Middle fifth	7130	6370
Next fifth	11 200	8610
Top fifth	19 750	13 480
All	8130	7370

UK Households 1984

SOURCE   *Social Trends, 1987* (London: HMSO, 1988).

How the Market Plays Fair

We could probably each decide our own version of a fair spread of wages. We could work out what we thought each person would deserve, no doubt quoting our own sterling qualities to place ourselves high on the list. And we would probably all disagree, for one person's view of what is fair is not the same as another's. One may rate compassion highly, another may prefer good humour. One may respect policemen, another may favour the clergy. Individual assessments such as these are purely subjective, and of no use to economists in explaining wage differences. Suppose, therefore, that we overcame our arguments about pay differences by agreeing that each worker should be paid exactly the same amount. Would this be fair?

There is one issue that runs through all pay assessments. Most people accept that pay should relate to the value of people's work. Harder work and more work deserves more pay. Someone who does no work at all deserves no pay. Pay is a reward for work done. So what happens if pay is now made regardless of the work done? Some people may look on work as a fulfilment in its own right and continue to do the best job they can. Their religion may encourage them to do so, as in Buddhism, for example, for the credit this brings them in afterlife. But the very fact that this is seen as being virtuous and unnatural suggests how much it goes against the way of the world. The sin of sloth may come more naturally to most of us, and we are more likely to choose to work less while others continue to do our work for us. The outcome of equal wages is not so much equal work as no work at all.

A free market economy leaves no room for conjectures such as these. It has its own unanswerable logic to decide the relative worth of workers and differences in pay. People do not matter; all that counts is the labour they offer for sale and its value in the market place. Marx wrote his, literally, world shattering book, *Das Kapital*, in the free enterprise world of Dickensian England. He wrote to a friend that 'it will not even pay for the cigars I smoked writing it'. The pay of each type of labour is decided by free market forces of supply and demand, that we met earlier. Broadly speaking, a worker is paid more if her/his type of labour is in high demand for its value in production to employers, and in low supply in the market place as a whole. Scarcity value sets relative pay. Workers are paid what they are worth in production. We can all argue about whether this is fair or not, but it is at least clear and objective.

Demand and Supply Set Pay

Economic analysis gives us the tools to explain differences in pay in the same way as with any other prices in any other markets. The demand for each type of labour depends on its value in production. Firms seek to employ labour by comparing each worker's production value with their cost, or rate of pay. A rise in pay means that fewer workers are worth employing, as expressed in terms of a movement along the demand curve for labour, described earlier. The supply of each type of labour, on the other hand, tends to rise as pay rises, as workers are attracted into this form of employment rather than another. Thus the supply curve behaved as seen earlier. Provided that other conditions do not change, these levels of offered demand and supply for each type of labour can be compared in the market place. Theoretically, these offers are compared at each possible level of wages, as shown in Figure 2.3.

If pay were to rise too high then more labour would be offered than firms could afford to employ. This would cause unemployment in the way we saw earlier. If pay were to fall too low, the opposite would happen and more jobs would be created than there were people to fill them. This would show up in overtime working, unfilled job vacancies and production bottle-necks. The behaviour of the supply and demand curves means that there is only one level of wages which is at just the right level to match supply with demand. Only the equilibrium level of pay clears the market. This is the level that the market will set. Anywhere higher and surplus labour pushes wages down; anywhere lower and unfilled job offers pull wages up.

Demand and supply set equilibrium wages for each type of labour, and differences in demand and supply in each part of the labour market explain the differences in pay that come about. Demand is based on the productive value of labour and the hard fact of economic life is that some workers are more productive, some are more commercially valuable, than others. Consider an assistant and his supervisor, for instance. The supervisor has more experience and responsibility and contributes more to their shared production. This may not be reflected in physical effort, of course, since most advanced work is more thoughtful than muscular. Consider also two artists who produce equivalent works of art but one is in fashion and commands a high price, while the other does not. It is the price of one's production that affects pay, and not just the amount, as Karl Marx knew to his cost.

There are supply differences also. Some types of labour are very common. Street cleaners require little skill or experience and are

FIGURE 2.3
Equilibrium Pay

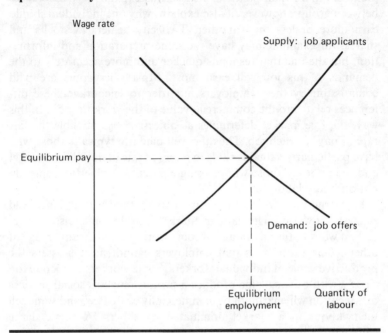

easily replaced. Airline pilots must have natural qualities such as eyesight, composure and judgement, plus years of technical training and experience. They are very difficult to replace. But some skilled areas of work now attract relatively large numbers of recruits, perhaps because of the nature of the work. The appeal of nursing or social work, for example, raises supply and depresses pay, while discomfort and unsocial hours deter workers from traditional manufacturing jobs. And supply can differ also just because of the location of jobs and workers: if people cannot afford to live close to jobs in London then supply is reduced and wages raised.

Rich and Poor

So what is it that separates the rich and the poor? In terms of wages earned from work done by labour, the answer is now clear. One type of labour earns more than another because of greater demand and/ or lesser supply. Thus brain surgeons earn more than seamen, plumbers more than painters. Just as this explains pay differences between groups, however, it also explains why one individual should earn more or less than another. Two city dealers in stocks and shares, for example, may have the same preparation and information, but the one that responds quicker and more accurately to the demands of his job will earn most. Most salespeople are paid commission by their employers in order to encourage these differences related to the commercial value of the work they do. In this way, the free market determines as objectively as possible the fair rate of pay for each job. Thus the well paid are typically those who have particularly valuable skills to offer for sale in the labour market and the poor are those who, as single parents or elderly people, do not offer any labour at all.

Pay structures are not as clear or as methodical as this would suggest, however. The labour market can become distorted in certain ways to the advantage of some workers, and disadvantage of others. One problem is that employers cannot always assess the productive value of individual workers. Some workers cooperate too closely with others, some produce a product such as social services or education which cannot be commercially evaluated, and some sell their labour in a market dominated by others. A single, large employer can set wages without reference to competitors knowing that the workers have no close, alternative jobs. The government may be the only employer of certain skills, in the police or army, and again have some freedom, at least for a while, to dictate employment terms. Thus pay levels may become distorted, to appear unrealistically high for some groups and too low for others.

Trade unions are also in the business of influencing relative pay. A strong union can restrict the supply of labour in its field, and make agreements with employers and other unions that reinforce the value of its members' work to their employers. Closed shops ensure that only the union's own members can take certain jobs, and make those members, in effect, irreplaceable by employers. All this may limit employment but it raises pay, for the union's own members at least.

Pay differences in practice, therefore, reflect a host of institutional influences. Collective bargaining between employers and unions limits the room for individual and more flexible arrangements and exaggerates the role of comparisons, precedents and relativities.

Habit and accepted practice can matter more than long-term, underlying pressures of supply and demand. Bargaining skill and political pressure can matter more than anything. All this may distort or disguise market pressure but not just for one group of labour against another. It affects also the relative earnings of different types of factors of production altogether – of labour against capital and those who own it.

Shirkers and Workers: A Reinterpretation

What are these other factor incomes? We saw in the last chapter how resources can be classified in economics as the four factors of production: land, capital and enterprise as well as labour. Each of these earns a return for its work in production in a similar way to labour, based on its scarcity value to employers. Labour may claim the lion's share of total national earnings but capital and land are owned by individuals also, and the personal earnings of these individuals are typically much greater. Successful entrepreneurs, who set up their own companies and earn profits from their operations over the years, stand to earn much more still. Thus the list of the nation's richest people includes no wage earners at all (Table 2.3). The rich have been born into wealth from their inheritance of land, stocks and shares or, more rarely, have made their own wealth from capital ownership. Once in that position, however, wealth generates more wealth as land, capital and enterprise earn rent, interest and profit in following years.

Where does this lead us in the distinction between people as shirkers or workers? Our starting point, stylised and prejudiced though it might have been, was that people have a free choice whether to enter work or remain unemployed. We have seen that this cannot be sustained, except perhaps for a relative few. Unemployed people are eligible for and looking for work by definition, but economic conditions in the labour market make too few jobs available. This may be because of the restrictive actions of unions, employers and government in keeping wages too high, in one view, or inadequate spending in the macroeconomy as a whole, in another. In either case, the unemployed individual has little chance to determine his own fate and is at the command of much greater, impersonal economic forces.

TABLE 2.3
The UK's Richest People

---

1. The Queen	£5200m	Inherited as head of state
2. The Duke of Westminster	£3200m	Inherited. Landowner including 300 acres of Mayfair
3. Lord Sainsbury and family	£1967m	Family control of 55% of the supermarket chain, founded in 1869
4. Gad and Hans Rausing	£1900m	Swedish tax exiles, own Tetra-Pak food packaging firm founded 1951
5. Sir John Moores	£1700m	Founder of Littlewoods Pools, Britain's largest private company

The richest 200 people own £38 billion, and at least £30 million each. They own 7% of the UK land mass, 35% are members of the House of Lords, and 57% inherited their wealth.

SOURCE   *The Sunday Times Magazine*, 2 April 1989.

But the earnings of each individual who is in employment also deserve careful interpretation. Labour earns on the basis of its scarcity value in the market place. This may be because of exceptional, personal qualities of hard work but is much more likely to be because of the productive capital equipment that the labour is allowed to work with, or the commercial value of whatever product the labour happens to be making. Individual people earn on the basis of their ownership of factors of production, and those who earn most typically have factors other than their own labour that they can put to work. They have to take decisions, they have to sign their own cheques, but the notion of hard work again seems to be a remote one.

Market economics provides us with an objective analysis of employment and earnings. But in that analysis there is no place for subjective, personal assessments of ideas such as hard work, fair play or shirking. In economics there are only workers and non-workers.

All's Fair in ...
Competition

3

'Corporate raiders', 'pacman defences', 'a white knight riding in to the rescue'. This is the stuff of war correspondents, or at least war games enthusiasts. But most battles are no longer fought on the beaches or the plains. Advanced industrial countries have their beaches fully occupied by sun-bathing tourists and their plains covered with warehouses and factories. Now the scene of battle is in the boardrooms and trading floors where business competition is at its fiercest.

The stakes in this game are enormous. Companies bid billions of pounds, more than the national incomes of whole countries, for the ownership of their rivals. Chevron paid $13 000 million for Gulf Oil in 1984. Youngsters used to enter business by starting on the shop floor, training on the job, learning how to create the product and satisfy the customer. Now the quickest route to the top bypasses the product and the customer altogether. High-flyers study at college till their mid-twenties, collect their MBA (Master of Business Administration) and earn their wings advising MDs (Managing Directors) which companies to take over, strip down, or sell off.

The Story of a Merger

Guinness was the standard-bearer for Britain's new, industrial competitiveness in the mid-1980s. The new chief executive, Ernest

Saunders, turned the company around in just four years. Guinness grew from being a one-product brewer with old-fashioned ideas and limited prospects to a multiproduct giant selling a full range of famous brand names. Its market valuation rose fortyfold. Its route to competitive success was acquisition, at a total cost of around £4 billion.

Saunders needed to buy competing drinks companies to diversify Guinness's product range and develop its market strength. There was a bitter but successful struggle to buy Bells, the Scotch whisky company, for £400 million. Then came the big one. The giant Distillers company, with a huge range of famous brands and different products, was resisting an unwelcome take-over bid from the Argyll Group. Guinness was welcomed as a 'white knight' with an alternative offer and succeeded in buying Distillers for a record £2695 million, in April 1986.

History was made and Guinness's competitive market position secured. But the story did not stop there. Guinness had bought the giant company with a cash and shares offer and rumours started to flow about the shares element in this. Over in America the Wall Street arbitrageur Ivan Boesky was facing charges of insider dealing and crooked market practices because of his abuse of privileged information to make a speculative fortune in the markets. When, inevitably, he started trading information it was the Guinness scandal that hit the fan. Just eight months after the take-over the merchant bankers responsible for Guinness's success resigned, and the relevant director resigned from his £300 000 job with them. The Department of Trade and Industry announced an investigation. Then the Finance Director, and two others, and Saunders himself left the Guinness board. What had been going on? It seems that Guinness, through its own merchant bank, had paid £7.6 million to another bank. That bank led its clients to buy Guinness shares during the take-over battle, and then bought them back afterwards at a substantial, rewarding premium. Other leading entrepreneurs and banks in London, New York and Switzerland played the same game. The effect was to keep the value of Guinness shares unrealistically high, while they were being offered as part of the take-over deal. But it is illegal for executives to spend a company's money on its own shares and it is a criminal offence to defraud the share market in this way.

Eighteen months after the take-over, charges were brought

against four of Britain's most successful businessmen. The scandal involved the best British banks, stockbrokers, managers and companies. Who knows how widespread such tactics were during the merger boom years of the 1980s? Ernest Saunders faced forty charges of £24 million theft, false accounting, conspiracy, illegal purchases, and intent to pervert the course of justice.

* * *

The significance of competition is reflected in the lengths firms go to avoid it. A direct rival in your market place threatens not just your sales but your income and your job. You must find less threatening ways to do business, keeping your own customers loyal to your product while tempting your competitor's from him. Better still, you should develop new products and new markets that are entirely yours so that no other firm competes there. You should discourage other firms from seeking to compete with you and put those who do out of business. The most certain way of doing this, of course, is to take them over so that you control all their operations and earn all their profits as well as your own. The only safe competition is no competition at all.

Companies that are successful, therefore, watch their competitors very closely. They want their rivals' customers and market share for themselves, and they want their products, their resources and their profits as well. As Dickens expressed it through the words of Jonas Chuzzlewit, brim-full of Victorian values, 'Do other men, for they would do you. That's the true business precept.' The lust for power is alive and well in the world of business. Indeed, it is an essential part of the competitive framework, and the starting point for our analysis of the economics of production.

What Do Companies Do?

Before being broken into eight parts Bell USA was worth around $150 000 million, and was owned by over 3 million shareholders. Other organisations are smaller and more anonymous to the general public due to the nature of their business or their name: ICT, IT, BOC, ICC, etc. But all these are what we think of as companies. They are production organisations set up as legal bodies in their own right, with shareholders, managers and employees. The shareholders together own the company through their purchase of a certificate representing a proportion of the original capital investment. They earn profits, if there are any, from the company's trading. They can sell and buy their shares in a large, public market, through the Stock Exchange.

Managers and workers are employed by the company as its labour. Managers are appointed, at top level by the shareholders' representatives on the Board of Directors, to run the company from day to day. They may own shares as well but their earnings are typically from regular salaries to reflect their seniority, perhaps with bonuses based on sales performance. The work of the company is entirely its own decision but the large, well-known ones usually deal in many different products, perhaps in quite different industries, in many different countries.

Most companies are neither large nor famous, however. For each multinational giant there are many more companies that trade in a small-scale, specialised way, perhaps with a workforce of only a few people, perhaps selling only one product in one country. The owners may all be part of the same family and the shares may never be offered or exchanged by the general public. Most companies start this way, setting up limited liability to protect their shareholders from unlimited risk in the case of failure.

Enter Economic Theory

The real world of business offers variety and confusion. For the purposes of economic theory, however, this will not do at all. Economic principles aim to explain, certainly, but also to clarify and predict. To make these clear predictions about the behaviour of companies, therefore, we must define exactly what types of business and decisions we are dealing with. Many students start their work in economics a little disappointed with this aspect of production theory: meeting principles and situations that seem to relate only imperfectly to the real world of business that they can observe around them. But patience is rewarded, for from that introductory analysis it is possible to proceed further and faster at more complicated and realistic study later. The value of simple models is in large part the training that they offer, as well as the specific conclusions they yield.

In terms of simple economic theory, we look at a rather simpler form of beast than the multinational, joint stock company. We study the rural peasant rather than the yuppie; knowing that one evolved from the other, is basically still the same, and can still find antecedents in parts of the world today. Our theoretical producer is a firm, producing just one product and selling in just one market. The firm is owned and run by the same individual so that decisions are taken only for the purpose of making profit: thus this firm is precisely entrepreneurial. The entrepreneur takes decisions for the firm from the basis of accurate and complete knowledge, not only about conditions within the firm itself but in the market place outside and for other firms and customers as well. Thus all decisions are rational rather than accidental, and all behaviour is predictable and profitable.

The firm must take decisions in three main areas. First, is the matter of how best to make its product. The aim must be to cut the cost of making each particular level of output as low as possible, but the conditions of supply will determine whether this implies low- or high-scale production, and the best mix of different factors of production. Secondly, there are questions about how best to sell the product, in terms of price and so forth, in the face of competition from other firms selling to the same customers in the same market. Lastly, there is the choice of production level, set in the best interests of the entrepreneur's profits. This also will be affected crucially by the state of competition with other firms. Economic principles show producers the way to approach decision-making, in terms of simple common sense at the very least, in all three of these areas.

How Best to Produce?

Entrepreneurs earn profit so it makes sense for them to run their companies aiming to make as much profit as possible. Profit is made from the excess of sales revenue over production costs, so the entrepreneur aims, we assume, to maximise this profit by making as much revenue as possible, but also by keeping costs as low as possible, at each level of output. But what is the best way to produce in order to keep costs this low? Obviously this will depend on the particular production conditions facing the firm, but there are some general principles to be identified.

A firm tries to combine its different factors of production together in the most efficient way. Efficiency in this context is a specific, commercial concept: achieving a given level of output at lowest possible cost. This affects the firm in very different ways, however, depending on the time allowed for adjustment. Suppose the firm considers just two of its inputs at first: labour and capital. It needs both to make its product but it is technically possible to achieve production with different arrangements of the two. Capital intensive production would use more machinery, perhaps robots on a production line, and relatively little labour to support it. Labour intensive production could produce as much but from many workers using much less, and less sophisticated equipment such as hand tools. The choice between different methods is made on the basis of the value for money offered by each factor. If labour is relatively cheap, but also reliably productive, it is a better 'buy' than capital. If capital equipment becomes less expensive then its value for money in production improves. Firms must continue to assess technical possibilities, factor costs and production figures to maintain their efficiency from least-cost production.

What is technically possible is not necessarily physically possible, however, at any given period of time. Time is an essential dimension here in deciding how a firm should produce. Capital equipment cannot all be quickly installed and skilled, experienced labour cannot be quickly hired or fired. Over a short-term period, therefore, while at least one factor of production cannot be adjusted, the firm has fewer options. It cannot alter all factors to keep costs as low as possible and has to change variable factors only, in combination with a fixed amount of at least one other. This introduces one of the most fundamental principles of economics: the law of diminishing returns. We all recognise the way that too many cooks spoil the broth, where ever-increasing inputs eventually bring less and less extra output. To firms this makes it harder to produce efficiently as output is increased in the short term exactly because additional factors such as labour tend to crowd fixed factors such as machinery.

Diminishing returns affect costs across the range of output levels in the way shown in Figure 3.1. This measures the average cost of producing each unit of a firm's output. Even at its best this cost will tend to be greater in the short term before more efficient factor

FIGURE 3.1
Costs in the Short and Long Term

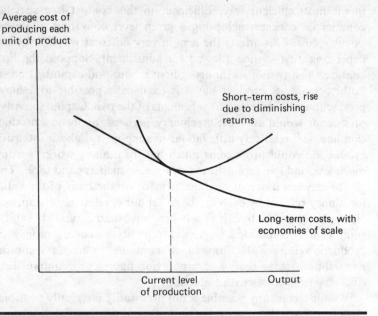

Average cost of
producing each
unit of product

Short-term costs, rise
due to diminishing
returns

Long-term costs, with
economies of scale

Current level
of production

Output

combinations become possible in the long term. But additional features of production may well exaggerate this difference. Many firms find that they can affect their productive efficiency by altering their scale of production. They change scale by adjusting employment of all inputs together, clearly only as a long-term decision taken when all factors are variable. Large-scale production can bring distinct advantages through the use of indivisible, heavy equipment, bulk buying, financial risk-spreading and so forth.

Economies of scale allow firms to cut average costs and improve efficiency. They arise when oil companies use supertankers or conglomerate, finance companies spread their risks by operating in many different fields at the same time. They explain why so many companies strive to grow in order to dominate their markets, undercut their rivals and boost profits. But they do not apply universally for there may come a point where a company grows too far and too fast, becomes difficult to manage, and suffers diseconomies of scale that raise average production costs. At the other end of the scale, there are clearly many areas of production where it pays to be small. Small firms may be able to adapt more sensitively to the demands of their customers. They may be able to serve more specialised markets, perhaps at a local level. They may be able to develop their own, new products and carve their own niche in the market place.

Prices and Marketing

It is one thing to make a product efficiently, but it is quite another to sell it successfully in the market place. In many companies these different functions require such different skills and information that they are performed by different people. Marketing is a complicated and diverse art that involves identifying and encouraging market demand, developing products, and selling effectively in terms of a range of qualities. In real world conditions, these selling qualities feature the nature of the product, especially new products, and distribution through resale outlets and promotion and advertising. But these aspects all imply that one firm's product differs in significant ways from its competitors; indeed, it is generally the purpose of the marketing exercise to develop that perception in the customer's mind. This is more than simple economic theory can cope with.

The principles of production are explained most clearly when firms compete in the same market to sell the same product. Thus each firm's product must be substantially the same, without advertising, or distribution or branding or packaging or development differences. But what else is left, you may ask, that firms can compete in? There is perhaps the most fundamental area of all: the price of the product itself. Everything else being equal, consumers will prefer the product they can buy at a lower price. This allows them to achieve more satisfaction from their given income. The firm that sells at a lower price sells more than its competitors, and achieves a larger share of the market. This is the stuff that marketing managers dream of.

How much more can a firm sell by cutting price? This is a crucial question for there would be little point in dropping price, and so forgoing sales revenue, if sales did not increase to claim back revenue. Firms must consider the competitive state of their market place. Perfect competition is the situation described by economists where a huge number of small firms all sell to the same market. If any firm raises its price above everyone else's then it sells nothing. If any firm drops its price it is overwhelmed with more orders than it can hope to meet. Firms do best by selling as much as they like all at the same market price. Imperfect competition is where firms have the ability to influence the going market price through their own price/output decisions. Now they can lower prices to increase sales, but they need to work out carefully the money both lost and gained from doing so. That leads us on to the last area for decisions, about how much it is best to sell.

Profit-maximising Output

The virtue of simple economic principles is illustrated best in the context of a firm's decision on output. Firms could choose any level at all out of the huge range of technical possibilities. They have to take into account the whole range of efficiency and marketing considerations that we have already surveyed. And yet the decision between production levels for a rational, entrepreneurial firm boils down to just one simple issue. This type of firm chooses the one level of output at which profits are greatest. There is only one such point, the available information on costs and sales revenue identifies it exactly, and the answer is incontestable.

Notice that this is true only because of the particular principles that apply along the way. Diminishing returns in production explain the rise in average costs, and market competition explains that price either remains constant (in perfect competition) or must be reduced (in imperfect competition) in order to increase sales. Thus there is a point at which the difference between revenue and costs is greatest, and if output is raised beyond that point then profits decline. But we also know that an entrepreneur takes decisions only for personal return, and that return is as profit only. So output is increased whenever that adds more to revenue than to costs and is cut whenever that saves more from costs than revenue. Output is set, therefore, where the addition to revenue exactly matches the addition to costs, at the profit-maximising point (see Figure 3.2).

Some readers may have noticed by this point, either from their

FIGURE 3.2
Profit-maximising Output

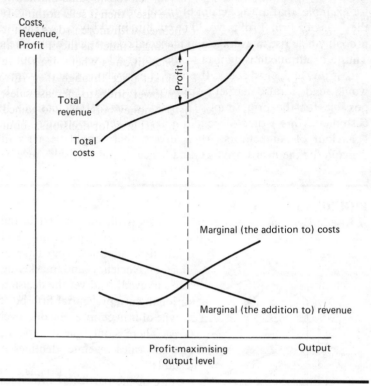

sympathy or horror of the subject, that there is a distinct undercurrent of mathematics running through all this. Additional cost and revenue is a marginal, incremental or, in mathematical terms, a differential measurement. The marginalist treatment of production theory (and there are many other areas of conventional economics that also use the same approach) was developed by economists in the last century, in terms of the new science of calculus then being developed. The advantage of such a mathematical approach is to express production conditions for efficiency and competition determinately, solve them simultaneously, and reach a single, maximised conclusion. We may disguise the maths involved in common-sense

terms and everyday examples but it is still implicit in the approach
and its results.

   How does this help us to predict the behaviour of firms? Suppose,
for example, that a wage claim or interest rate rise were to increase
the costs of a firm. Profits would be cut but, in addition, there would
probably be a rise in average and marginal costs at all output levels.
Thus a profit maximising firm would prefer a lower level of output
and, if this happened across the market as a whole, reduced supply
would tend to raise market price for the product. It would not be
possible for the firm simply to pass on its cost increase to its
customers: this would depend on its market situation and the
behaviour of competitors. Alternatively, there might be a rise in
demand for the firm's product, and hence its possible sales revenue

FIGURE 3.3
A Rise in Demand

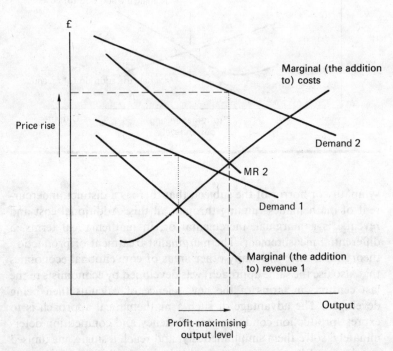

at each sales level. Here the firm would maximise profits by raising output and, depending on the competition again, the price of its product. Figure 3.3 shows this latter situation, with output set in each case where marginal cost equals marginal revenue, and price set by the demand for that output.

Compete or Die

Firms are in competition with each other when they try to sell identical products to the same group of consumers, or try to employ factors from the same group of suppliers. This competition takes different forms, as we have already seen. Perfect competition is an extreme and perhaps purely theoretical case where firms must choose to sell their identical products at the same market price. The market for shares or newspapers sold from shops may be very like this. But there are many more markets around where firms all seem to sell at much the same prices, despite an absence of the necessary conditions of perfect competition. Why is this?

Consider the competition between petrol companies, or banks or supermarket chains. Here there are a handful of main companies in each market, but they all set much the same, and often exactly the same prices for what they sell. This could look deceptively like perfect competition but for the small number of firms, and the other ways in which they behave. Competition between a few sellers is called oligopoly, and is characterised by non price competition. Suppose you were shopping around for a new car and every dealer kept to the same price. You would soon appreciate the opportunities for 'free' features such as radio or sunroof, delivery, full petrol tank, warranty and servicing. These are all examples of non-price competition and firms in oligopoly are usually much keener to offer them than to drop price. Price cuts damage sales figures and profits but more importantly they can prompt retaliation from competitors. Firms lose sales revenue if they all cut price together, but any firm who raises price is only likely to lose out as well when undercut by competitors. Better not to change price at all, if they can manage it.

What we observe, therefore, is that firms compete in a real world monopoly game. Each wants the others' factors, products, customers and market share for itself. It uses whatever means might legally and effectively capture those targets. It trades areas of specialisation within its markets in order to build economies of scale. It competes strongly, and even at a loss, with newer, smaller firms to expell them from the market, then lifts its price to earn profit. At the same time, it uses advertising, product development and promotion to maintain its customers' brand loyalty. Much of this benefits consumers through low prices or new and better products, or efficient distribution and service. Thus the process of competition can be a positive influence. But the final target that motivates much of this behaviour is to dominate and control the whole market, and to acquire all that is your competitors'. If ever that end is reached, with a monopoly being the only seller in its market, then customer service and value for money will quickly become secondary considerations behind the lust for profit.

The Human Factor

The predictions of production theory are clear, simple and unambiguous, in fact most unlike what is typically observed in the real world. There firms' decisions can be inconsistent and unpredictable at times. Information about costs and sales is often imperfect, especially when it concerns competing firms or potential customers. Even highly efficient firms may be unable to measure the cost or revenue of individual, additional units of output because these measures are shared by a batch of production. Where information does exist it may lead to different interpretations of policy for the short as opposed to the long term. Short-term profits may be possible at the expense of investment for the long term.

Missing in all this, as well, is the human dimension. Firms are run by people, and decisions are taken on the basis of habit, hunch and individual motivation, as well as for the profits of the company. To understand the behaviour of firms properly it is necessary to understand how people behave within their social organisation, and how decisions are made within collective enterprises. The starting point in all this is to distinguish the roles of shareholders, managers and workers, for only in the smallest and most entrepreneurial of firms do all three become interrelated. Most large companies are owned by one group of people and investing institutions, but run by a largely different group of paid employees. The information, motivation and behaviour of one group is very likely to differ from that of the other. In particular, the managers will be motivated to keep their jobs by providing enough profit to satisfy shareholders, but thereafter to pursue targets of their own. The course of the firm's behaviour is likely to alter as a result.

What do managers do, therefore, and how may their decisions be influenced by the human factor? Some people work for companies as professional experts, as accountants, lawyers or surveyors, say, much as if they were independent and self-employed. The firm claims allegiance and specialised knowledge, but otherwise employs professionals for their expertise. Managers in large corporations also specialise to a large extent, providing their firm with economies of scale from the use of experts. Management functions are often divided between production matters, financial control and marketing and sales. Someone who enters, trains and practises in one area may never transfer to another. General managers are needed to supervise and coordinate all these functions together, but even at the top, in the Board of Directors, there are likely to be specialised responsibilities allocated to the Financial Director, Sales Director, and so forth.

Separate functions lead to some measure of conflict, although the company will aim to ensure that this is constructive and cooperative conflict, between management groups. Production responsibilities include technical work to maintain machinery, order inputs, employ labour effectively and control quality. This may embrace other specialisations such as research and development into products and processes, and personnel management. These managers focus on their product, plants and workforce. Very different work is involved in marketing the product, by researching the tastes and consumption patterns of customers, delivering the product to distributors, and preparing it in a form, at a price that will sell best. This may conflict directly with financial controls of costs, efficiency and profits, which involve financial specialists at each stage of production and sales within the company.

Decision-making Skills

It is clear that the potential for confusion in the behaviour of large organisations is enormous. Could one individual or group in a company gain the power to send it stumbling off course, therefore, like some great rogue elephant, to pursue campaigns and vendettas against its competitors? Could someone with a lust for power find a way to distort the behaviour of a company for his personal gain? It seems most unlikely, for a number of reasons. The first is that managers are trained in the art of decision-making. Good decision-making involves supervision and a coalition of interests which keep individual excesses in check. Managers are professional decision-makers.

The decision-making process is systematic (see Figure 3.4). It starts by defining a problem that needs solving, a question that needs an answer. Next there must be information about that problem, collected fully and accurately. From this it is possible to have consultation of interested parties to collect opinions and points of view. Finally, comes the point of decision, based on background knowledge of information and interests, but followed up later with feedback and appraisal in case the system of decision-making might be improved in future. This procedure can apply to decisions in any organisation and any walk of life, but managers know that they must be expert at it if they are to succeed in their careers. Thus they develop the skills needed to support it, dealing with people to get the best from them, presenting and interpreting data, guiding meetings efficiently towards appropriate conclusions.

Efficient, well-trained managers are even more likely to divert from company shareholders in terms of motivation and behaviour, however, if their targets for personal satisfaction differ significantly. Managers measure their success probably in terms of the size of their responsibility, numbers of employees, status within the company hierarchy, and so forth. This is likely to relate more to the scale of total budget or the growth of sales than to the profitability of the operation alone. Managers increase their salaries by moving on to larger, higher jobs in the same or another company. Their first concern is to meet profit targets set by shareholders, through the board, but after that they are free to follow more individual targets for growth, and the size of their own section of the business.

Why do the shareholders tolerate this? If you owned shares in a company you would either sell them or vote to sack the management if you did not receive the maximum possible profit, wouldn't you? Well you might try to, but only if you knew what that potential level was and, in a situation of limited competition and limited information, you are most unlikely to do so. Furthermore, shareholders

FIGURE 3.4
The Decision-making Process

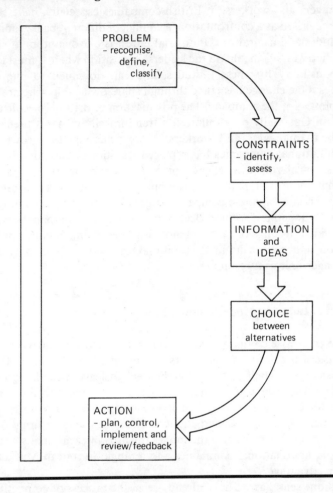

invest in shares not just for one year's profits but for long-term earnings, and for capital gain. They buy at one price hoping to sell at a higher price, so gaining in terms of the value of their capital investment. Company growth, especially at the expense of market competitors, promises well for future profits and therefore the value of the shares. Shareholders want their companies to reinvest profit and develop strong growth and sales policies.

There have been times when relationships between shareholders, managers and workers, in British companies especially, have been characterised as a confrontation, a conflict of different backgrounds, attitudes and aspirations. Industrial unrest is one symptom of such conflict. Management is in the leadership position where it must take responsibility for these attitudes, and can do much to improve things. One change has come through share ownership schemes for employees of the company. The privatisation of British Telecom and British Gas really only followed a trend in selling shares preferentially to managers and workers. More generally, the growth of multinational companies has replaced traditional, class-dominated divisions of role with a new spirit of cooperation and allegiance within many companies. This approach, so much a feature of German and Japanese companies especially, encourages employees to work together for the collective interests of the company, despite individual feelings or personal motives. There is much more consultation and consensus in decision-making, and the company is a stronger unit as a result.

British Industry Under Competition

Free enterprise companies are driven to compete with each other in the quest for markets, customers and profits. Managers take these decisions on behalf of their shareholders, at least in the long term, and so decide how to produce, how to market their products and how to set price and output at the best levels. But how do British producers fare in this competitive environment against firms from the rest of the world? Are the moves towards international specialisation, multinational companies and a Single European Market to their advantage?

In one sense, as we have already seen, the process of competition is distinctly advantageous to consumers as a whole and the producers who satisfy them best. Successful firms are those that develop the best new products, market them most attractively and produce them most efficiently. The remarkable growth of international trade and the pace of technological progress in recent years has allowed for enormous economies of scale and rearranged rationalised production. British living standards benefit from this specialisation in trade, and successful British companies lead the way in their world markets. But there is another side to the coin as out of-date, small-scale production fails in this hard, competitive world. Imported motor-bikes and videos have so much to offer in terms of perform-ance and price that British producers cannot compete and go out of business almost entirely. British cars, washing machines and foo-twear face the same threat.

These are all examples of manufacturing production, which makes finished, tangible goods out of basic, raw materials. The conventional image of industry, showing smoking chimneys and production line factories is of exactly this type. In Britain, it is this manufacturing industry which is so much under fire from internat-ional competition. The last ten years have seen a traditional balance of payments surplus turn to deficit on trade of this type. The measure of total, real output of manufacturing goods has risen only a little, and by far less than for national output as a whole (see Table 3.1). Around one in every three jobs in manufacturing industry has disappeared, probably never to be seen again. Some of these changes

---

TABLE 3.1
UK Manufacturing and Services

	1960	*1979*	*1986*
Share of Manufacturing in Total Output (%)	32.1	24.9	21.8
Share of Manufacturing in Total Employment (%)	36.0	29.3	22.5
Index of Manufacturing Output (1980 = 100)	77.2	109.5	104.7
Employment in Manufacturing (000s)	8996	7253	5243
Employment in Services (000s)	11 362	13 580	14 192
Balance of Trade in Manufactures (£million)	+ 1552	+ 2698	− 8055
Balance on Invisible Trade Account (£million)	+ 173	+ 2713	+ 7607

SOURCE *Economic Trends, Annual Supplements* (London: HMSO).

may reflect an overdue rebuilding of leaner and fitter industries, but it is the last condition of an absolute loss of manufacturing jobs that gives the phenomenon its defining characteristic, as deindustrialisation.

Does Deindustrialisation Matter?

Most of the nation's production is not in manufactured goods and most jobs are outside manufacturing industry. We might import all we need of better, cheaper manufactured goods and concentrate on other types of work. There is no reason why the decline in manufacturing industry should be a worry, necessarily; but it is, all the same. The other sectors of production are of extracted raw materials such as foodstuffs, coal and oil in primary industries, and the production of services such as banking, entertainment and distribution in tertiary industries. These may produce more output and employ more people, but in other respects they cannot replace manufacturing.

Manufactures seem to gain almost infinitely from technical progress and economies of scale, developing new products and processes of production in a continuing and dynamic sequence of growth. This is reflected in international trade where most trade, and most trade growth is in terms of manufactured goods. Certain types of services may be able to offer similar qualities but Britain's experience suggests that it will be very difficult to replace manufactures in trade – especially within what is now the dominant market in Europe – as a growth inducing sector, or perhaps even in terms of new jobs for old.

Economists are concerned also that deindustrialisation occurs as a symptom of other, deeper problems. Free market forces are supposed to work through the process of competition to discourage inefficient production, but also to encourage the transfer of resources into new and more efficient areas. Competition ensures survival of the fittest in the economic jungle, and Britain should be able to find its own champions, in some industrial species or other, to survive when others perish. Either these market forces are being constrained and impeded, by government presumably, or they are too deeply flawed ever to work at all.

British governments in the 1980s took the view that free competition would itself improve efficiency and lead to the only possible long-term improvement in industrial performance. Policy, therefore, concentrated on removing government regulation and support, especially of weaker and nationalised industries. Tax advantages and enterprise packages were there to help new sectors compete successfully against continuing, even increasing international pressures. Reduced government borrowing released funds, in principle, for investment in these growth areas.

Left-wing critics pointed to the continued hardships in manufacturing, and its areas of concentration in the Midlands and North, as evidence for an alternative approach. They saw the failure of free, competitive forces as being endemic and unavoidable. Competitive failure leads to deflation, low spending and low investment, hence poor quality production of manufactures and repeated competitive failure. The only solution to this vicious circle, they said, was for the government to intervene directly. This could take the form of direct investment in industry and industrial areas, protection against foreign competition at least for a time, and reflation to reverse the cycle of decline. Clearly, this would conflict directly with the principles of free trade and competitive market forces, but that would really be the whole point. It would also be incompatible with membership of the European Community.

Merger Mania

One response that firms can make to the pressure of competition, especially when that pressure threatens to become overwhelming as it has for sections of manufacturing industry, is to merge. Mergers can be arranged, rather like weddings, in differing ways. Some happen by free and mutual consent, as a meeting of equals. Others are arranged by the parents for the good of the families and in what is seen as the best interests of both parties. A few are shot-gun affairs where one takes the other against their will. Whether as a merger, take-over or affiliation the motives for joining together usually fall into a pattern that is double-sided in its intentions and effects.

One side of the argument is for efficiency. Large firms can claim economies of scale in production, and also look for inspiration towards more dynamic growth and spin-offs that generate new ideas, new opportunities. The bundle of policies bringing a Single

European Market from 1992, for example, promote just this sort of thinking in major European companies. They face a larger and more accessible market for their products, but by combining with other European firms can produce and sell more efficiently throughout the Community. Hence the tendency towards rationalisation, closures and mergers, cutting employment in order to maintain current production more efficiently but also sponsoring growth and development which creates new jobs in future.

The other side of the case is less creditable. Two firms who compete directly and intensely with each other in one market can eliminate that competition at a stroke if they just merge together, pooling their resources, their products, their customers and their (greatly increased) profits. Mergers and take-overs can be purely defensive, therefore, to allow companies to avoid the insecurity, efficiency and consumer sovereignty imposed by competition. At the extreme, a monopoly firm is the only seller to its market. It can restrict supply to raise price and cut costs, knowing that consumers in that market have no close alternative that they can transfer to for satisfaction of their wants. It can find whatever combination of price and output brings in maximum profit, or choose instead to enjoy an easy life where inefficiency and high price prompts no retaliation from competitors.

Different types of mergers are likely to tend one way or the other between these two effects. Vertical mergers integrate firms at different stages in the production of the same good and stand to gain substantially from technical and marketing economies. But very few mergers are of this type. Many more involve horizontal integration between competing firms at the same stage in the same industry. Close competitors may also improve their efficiency, but cannot fail to reduce the number of firms selling against one another in the market place. Conglomerate companies are the result of diversification, which builds financial and managerial strength but also market influence and competitive power. Most of the largest companies and largest mergers these days involve conglomerates such as these.

Survival of the Fittest or a Lust for Power?

The twin paths followed by mergers towards efficiency and monopoly leave the government firmly stranded. They wish to protect consumers from anti-competitive practices while encouraging efficiency and rationalisation so that the country's industries can compete internationally. So should their policy be in favour of mergers or against them?

The inevitable compromise is to consider each case on its merits, and to investigate through the Office of Fair Trading and the Monopolies Commission only those, large proposals that give cause for public concern. The pressure of international competition and movement towards the Single European Market from 1992 makes national monopolies much less of a concern. They now face open competition with other countries' national monopolies in their turn. We can expect a continuing trend of mergers and take-overs to unite large companies into even fewer giant ones. The government has never really done very much to deter or control mergers in the past, but we can now expect its approach to become even more benign.

This should not mislead us into too rosy-eyed a view of corporate growth, however. Asset strippers will continue to search for bargain buys where the purchase of a majority of shares, even at a cost measured in millions of pounds, can pay for itself almost immediately through company closures and property sales. Market leaders will continue to buy up present or potential competitors in order to protect their position and keep captive their consumers.

Free competition through market forces has its justification in economics for the way it imposes a discipline of efficiency. Efficient companies produce cheaply, compete successfully and sell at a profit. Inefficient companies sell expensive, low quality products, do not compete, and are forced out of business through low profit. Survival of the fittest rewards efficient firms and banishes the inefficient. In this way, competition serves the best interests of consumers in general and the national economy as a whole.

But managers have the motivation and can gain the authority to use the competitive process in a lust for power. Large firms may undercut efficient competitors at a loss until, with greater resources, they win their market all for themselves. The lust for power is then rewarded through monopoly profits and security. Corporate Don Juans can raid the shareholdings of smaller companies in a similar way, for instant company growth, asset speculation rather than long-term production, or financial retaliation. There are many who disapprove of competition who nevertheless are happy to benefit from its advantages. The human experience suggests that it is unlikely to fade away. To quote a Victorian chant:

> Thou shalt not covet, but tradition
> Approves all forms of competition.

Market-making

4

Nothing provides a more powerful focus for people's differing attitudes towards the economic world than the behaviour of markets. Some see them as an elegant and efficient mechanism for distribution, and an opportunity for challenging analysis and sober, rewarding recreation – rather like doing *The Times* crossword. Others see them as a no-holds-barred street fight where personal greed is the only winner in a contest as sophisticated and challenging as a cross between Bingo and mud-wrestling.

How quickly the common image of markets has changed. Only a generation ago the term 'market' would have brought to mind a rural, Thomas Hardy world of gaily painted wagons covered by striped awnings, country town squares, and weekly trading of home-grown vegetables and teacloths. Certainly these markets existed, bringing together buyers and sellers to exchange goods and services in a social setting based on the community and its values at that time. Street markets continue today, of course, but the media have brought more technical markets into the public eye. Now we think of markets as TV images of monitors and phones, of angry youths yelling bids at one another for multitudes of dollars, or coffee options, or shares. The trading desks of the City now typify market dealing for many people and imply quite different social groupings and values.

This also has changed quickly. Work as 'something in the City' has always been associated with quick and ready money, but it used to involve well-educated, well-heeled men from only the better class of family and golf club. The old school tie and club atmosphere ensured standards where blackballs against unsuitable insurance underwriters could continue alongside the Stock Exchange pledge that 'my word is my bond'. This old world has been submerged in only a decade or so by a new City, in the public imagination at least, populated by ambitious and avaricious yuppies. They succeed through merit, by hard work and good fortune, and success means everything. Background and playing by the rules has become largely irrelevant in the open, competitive world of international dealing. Money is the common language and profit the common standard.

Getting Rich Quick

What connects these two worlds, of traditional street market trading and modern high finance dealing? In terms of economic principles and essential skills there is really a surprisingly large amount. A teenage barrow boy stands at his stall and yells his message to passing customers to advertise his wares. He has in mind the state of the rest of the market and especially the offers and the prices of other traders selling his sorts of goods. He is always on the make, offering to buy at a low price anything that he thinks he will be able to sell at a higher price. He sets price to make a profit on the turn around, but also to keep in with the rest of the market, attracting sellers and buyers in turn. If he finds that he is holding too much for too long he drops his asking price to attract buyers. If he is short of stock he bids a higher price to increase his supplies.

In terms of approach and strategy all this relates to City dealing just as much. It is only the scale of the business and the nature of the produce that differs. At best the barrow boys of the City can trade their way up to a fortune in no time, as many did in the boom years of the 1980s. Rising or 'bull' markets for property, stocks and shares meant that prices rose persistently, for years at a time. Any broker, such as an estate agent for housing property for instance, gains from a fixed percentage take on each deal when prices are rising. City dealers could do better still as they bought shares one day in order to sell at their regular profit the next, only to find prices rising by the time they sold, at even greater profit.

The 'Big Bang' in the City allowed new institutions to set up as advisers, and dealers, and investors in stocks and shares. The quickest way to combine what had previously been separated areas of expertise was, in 1986 and 1987, to merge traditional City firms. In the boom markets and new opportunities of that time, therefore, there was even more to be made for partners, shareholders and specialist dealers from selling out to these new conglomerates. The traditions of hundreds of years came second to the need to compete efficiently in international finance, and by the way, cash in the chips of ownership and expertise for millions of pounds.

The effect of these frantic events in the City on the rest of the economy was mixed. The City boom spun off into spending and investment around the South-East of England, but also into imported Porsches and Portuguese villas. Rising share prices and property values cascaded into a housing boom and credit expansion in the rest of the economy. But the example set by the new market-makers led to a more general awareness also of the power and significance of markets. To some, the impression was mainly one of selfish and uncaring greed. To others, these markets were seen as standard-bearers of the free enterprise system, performing a necessary and valuable function, allocating specialised goods and services from sellers to buyers on a colossal scale with speed and efficiency.

Perhaps both points of view carry some truth, and are not incompatible. Selfish greed is necessary as the motivation for market-makers to bring buyers and sellers together. It is the force that drives markets to clear immediately and exactly, keeping all parties satisfied with their transactions. This is indeed a remarkable and wondrous outcome, but one that we tend to take for granted in our familiar, free market world. Let us consider, therefore, how it is that market-makers do this work, and what general principles lie behind the behaviour of market price and quantity.

Making Markets

The theory of markets draws a simple, hypothetical model that represents the typical and essential features of the real world. Thus we consider one type of good where the amount offered for sale is the amount bought up, all at one market price. This matching quantity is achieved at that level of price and no other. But such a final outcome can actually be achieved only after natural market forces have played their part. The interest for an economist lies not in describing the end result but in explaining and predicting it. It is the economic story behind the apparent event which can be told another time with different characters in a different situation.

Put two characters into an Arabian bazaar, haggling over a magic carpet. Its wizened owner offers to sell for 200, so the brash young tourist offers 50. Both despair and turn away, then reconsider: 'I'll take 150' – 'I can buy another over there for 75.' Finally, they reach a deal at 110, and both leave well satisfied. This sort of dealing shows something of their plans and offers for the good. The stall holder is a market-maker in that he takes goods from suppliers and holds them, offering them for sale to buyers at a place and time, in a form in which they can buy. He may know that goods such as the carpet sell for 100 or more. He will offer to sell at any price he can get above that level, and if prices rise he will try to get more to sell. The buyer knows how much he wants the good and what he is willing to pay. Perhaps he could stretch even to 250, but if he sees the prices being paid in the market he will know how little he could spend elsewhere. If prices rise he has to cut down on how much he can get for his money.

This is bargaining between individuals. Our interest in markets as a whole is more general, and involves many buyers and sellers brought together only by their interest in the good being exchanged. As above, however, our focus is on the way signals reflect plans and intentions and how those intentions are reconciled. We assume that buyers and sellers act rationally on the basis of full and accurate information about their own circumstances and the state of the market at large. They make as much as they can of their own satisfaction and profits respectively. Thus their decisions over a given period of time are subject to predictable, common principles: the principles of demand and supply.

Demand and Supply

Economists explain the behaviour of any market in terms of the forces of demand and supply. These forces do not correspond exactly with the buying and selling decisions observed, for instance, in an eastern bazaar. Demand represents all the offers to buy, which may or may not be taken up in the market, as influenced by many different factors. Crucial among those factors is the market price. Other influences may differ from case to case and at first these are assumed to remain unchanged. But a high price discourages demand because buyers can only afford to buy less of the good, and find alternatives more attractive. A low price encourages demand.

Conversely, supply shows sellers' intentions in the market and, while other influences remain unchanged, is affected by price in the opposite way. A high price encourages sellers who stand to earn more on each sale, while a low price discourages all and may put some out of business altogether. A high price, therefore, induces more supply and less demand so leading to overselling and a buyers' market. Excess supply shows up as unsold goods until sellers drop their prices and buyers bid less to close the gap. A low price sets up low supply but high demand, hence a shortage and sellers' market. Buyers compete with each other to bid prices up and sellers increase their profits by marking up scarce goods. Shortages raise prices to close the gap between supply and demand.

So there is an automatic process of adjustment to match demand and supply through price adjustment. The motivation of buyers to obtain as much as they can for their money, and of sellers to earn as much profit as they can from their sales ensure that this process happens immediately and exactly in response to any observed shortage or glut. Thus an equilibrium price is established and, for given market conditions, shows no tendency to change. Demand is matched to supply at the same level of quantity both offered for sale and taken up. This is the situation shown in Figure 4.1.

Any change to market conditions registers in either demand or supply, or perhaps both. This alters the plans, the offers made to the market, and the equilibrium price and quantity. The amount of adjustment needed here differs from case to case, of course, especially in relation to the sensitivity of market forces to any given change in price. In general, the direction of change will be consistent, however, and reflected in shifts in the demand and supply curves drawn on a diagram such as Figure 4.1. An increase in demand at each price level, for example, raises consumers' intentions to buy. More demand leads to a shortage in the market. Price rises to its new equilibrium, but a higher price also encourages greater supply. Thus the end result can be predicted to be a rise in both price and quantity. In terms of the standard diagram this is represented as a

FIGURE 4.1
Market Equilibrium

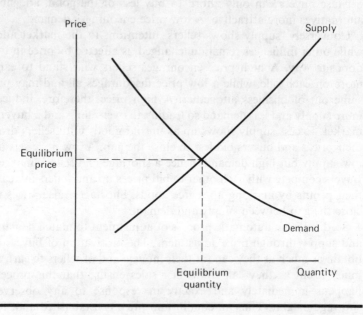

shift to the right, at each level of price, of the market demand curve. We can compare the old and the new equilibria, and the implied changes in price and quantity, as shown in Figure 4.2.

Reading the Crash

Notice that there are two stages to this treatment. One is to explain how equilibrium is set in a market as the forces of supply and demand respond to glut or shortage automatically, adjusting price to match selling and buying intentions. The other is to read a change in market conditions in terms of a direct shift to either demand or supply, and hence the adjustment from an old to a new equilibrium. Putting these stages to work we can predict the likely impact of a rise in demand, as above, which lifts both price and quantity in the market. Similarly, the theory shows that increased supply leads to a

FIGURE 4.2
A Shift in Market Demand

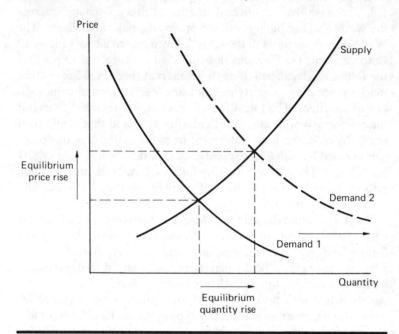

glut, and higher quantity but at a lower price. Conversely, lower demand brings lower price and quantity, and lower supply brings lower quantity at a higher price. There is a strong theme of common sense in all this, and the general lessons of market theory are accepted as facts of life by dealers such as those in the City. An understanding of market principles is a qualification for entry, in effect, to the job. Dealers know that a rush of interest from buyers, perhaps into pounds because inflation is down or interest rates up, means a rise in its price on the foreign exchanges. They know that a new government issue of bonds means a lower price for each one, and a greater rate of return on this form of investment. They know that a discovery of oil reserves will increase the profitability of the lucky oil company, leading to a rise in demand for and market price of its shares. In fact, if so many buyers and sellers understand these general principles so well one wonders that they ever get their fingers burnt at all, playing with the fires of the national economy.

In 1988, however, in what is since known as Black October, many did. The crash that hit prices then affected Stock Exchanges across the world, wiping billions off the prices of stocks and shares. The Wall Street share index in the USA fell by a record 22 per cent on 19 October alone, the FT index in Britain fell by its record 12 per cent the following day. The falling 'bear' market then spread into other markets, affecting property and housing, currencies and commodities to an extent. The forest fire of depression threatened to engulf the economic world rather as it did after 1929 and that Wall Street crash. By luck, and good judgement from the authorities, this panic was avoided but still a large number of City dealers had their fingers badly burnt. The effects in the City following the crash and Big Bang reforms were felt for a number of years in job losses, closures and market restructuring.

What was it that caused the 1988 crash, therefore, and why could such expert students of market economics as those in the City not foresee and avoid it? Perhaps some did but were bound up in a perfectly competitive field where none could afford to depart from market price. With foresight they all see that forces of demand and supply would turn price rises into price falls at some stage. Share prices rise when earnings from this type of investment, from profits, are expected to rise, making shares more attractive than alternative investments such as property or government bonds. But shares have an advantage over many other investments, and certainly those of loans to banks and building societies, because any price rise yields a capital gain in addition to straightforward earnings from dividends. Thus demand for shares will rise if cither profits are expected to improve or if share prices are expected to rise further.

The boom time conditions in 1987 and 1988 fulfilled both these expectations. Privatisation issues of shares in BP, Oil, Gas and Telecom furthered the trend of prosperity. Budgetary tax cuts, credit expansion and share-ownership incentives boosted spending, profits and investment yet again. But share and property prices rose by more than could be justified from expected investment returns alone. Prices were rising on the expectation of further price rises alone. Once this expectation reversed, the bubble would burst as it did in October 1988.

The fall in prices hit some dealers hard. Those with large holdings of shares they had bought in expectation of selling at higher prices now found they could only sell for much less. The loss of business, with less buying and selling altogether, hit harder still. There was less to be earned in commission and less work to employ all those engaged after Big Bang. Outside the City, however, there was little show of sympathy. Those who had lived by the market in the boom now died by the market in the crash. But there are other types of market that can be of much wider significance and affect us all. Some of these also suffer huge variations.

The Roof Over Your Head

One of the most basic of wants is for living accommodation, for the roof over your head. The market for owner-occupied housing, however, is one that has seen almost equal disruption in price and quantity as that for shares. In a boom time people can borrow on mortgage almost more than the value of the house they wish to buy, and more than they can easily afford to repay. They do so in the expectation, sometimes realised, that house prices can double in just a few years, giving property investors the greatest capital gain most could ever imagine, and a step along the inflationary house price ladder. As an added bonus, house buyers receive favoured treatment from the taxman in the form of tax deductions on mortgage interest payments. This prompted housing booms over a couple of periods in the 1980s. Those who took to heart the government's championing of a property-owning democracy, and very many did in the 1980s especially, gained substantial investment return, and a home to live in as well.

The house price boom was induced by rising demand. Partly this followed from the tastes of the population to buy rather than rent, and to live independently rather than as families. Mainly it followed from low real interest rates and preferential terms for mortgages. When people are offered the chance, through rising real incomes in an economic boom, they prefer to spend on their housing than almost anything else. But then comes the crunch. The government moves to choke off inflationary pressure by raising interest rates, but the first impact of that is felt by mortgage borrowers. Higher repayments deter house buyers and cut the amount they can afford for housing. Demand drops in the housing market as shown in

Figure 4.3. The tendency is for house prices to fall and sales quantity to fall as well, as a result.

Things are a little more complicated than this in real life, however. One problem is that existing home owners, and especially those who have just taken out 100 per cent mortgages to the limit that they can afford, are caught badly by the higher interest rates on their loans. In their tens of thousands they find that they just cannot afford the increased repayments and must sell their new homes. This increased selling only makes the market even more depressed. But potential sellers do not readily respond to this by cutting their asking prices. Many prefer to delay moving, and leave their property on the market for longer while waiting for the all-elusive buyer to come their way. So prices may be slow to fall and the market may be slow

---

FIGURE 4.3
Higher Interest Rates Cut House Prices

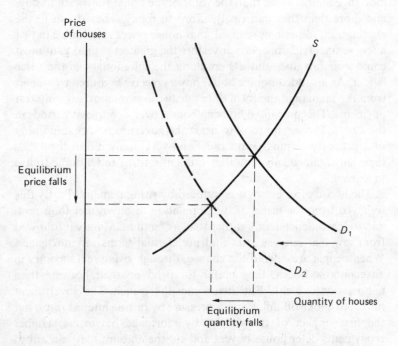

to clear. It may be some time before house sales and house prices recover.

The Pound in Your Pocket

It is difficult to grow up with money, knowing it from our earliest contact with economics, then reconciling such deep familiarity with the jargon and technicality of the foreign exchange markets. Is this stuff being measured in percentage points, at forward rates. at different values each day really the same as the money we all know and trust? Do the changes on the trading floors for long bonds, reserve currencies and sterling futures have any significance for the value of the pound in your pocket? Unfortunately they do, for the pounds involved are the same, and valuable for the British goods and services they can be exchanged for. But the reasons for dealing in these pounds may indeed change substantially on the journey these pounds take from the dealing rooms of the City to your bank account, purse or pocket.

The foreign exchange market brings together buyers and sellers of all the different national and international currencies of the world. You exchange your pounds in shops for goods and services, but foreign exchange dealers exchange pounds for dollars, deutschmarks, yen and other currencies. Each currency can be used to buy goods and services in its home country, and the main reason for currency exchange is to pay for the trade in those goods and services from one country to another. French firms need pounds instead of francs to pay for their import of British tea, tobacco and other products. British tourists need francs instead of pounds to pay for their hotels, travel and other expenses on holiday in France. So the demand for British currency depends essentially on the international demand for British exports, and the supply on British imports. City dealers undertake these purchases and sales on behalf of companies, banks and individuals.

There are other, more technical reasons for currency exchanges. Investors move capital from one country to another, as when Unilever UK, for example, buys the shares of a French perfume company, or builds a new factory in France for that company. Speculators hold their money in bank accounts in whichever currency seems to offer the best prospects of return. Too much

inflation, or a drop in interest rates, or a threat to the exchange rate
and they can quickly transfer funds out, often on a colossal scale.
The government itself holds foreign currencies in its official reserves.
These also can be substantial, at times over 10 per cent of national
income. Their use is for the government to create its own demand or
supply of currencies artificially, for no other reason than to influence
the international value of the pound whenever it wishes to do so.

Exchange Rate Fluctuations

Buying and selling in the foreign exchange market sets the exchange
rate of the pound. The main measure quoted is the Effective
Exchange Rate index, which takes the value of the pound against a
weighted average of other major currencies. A rise in the exchange
rate might once have been welcomed as a sign of international
esteem, but now its effects on economic performance are what
matter. A higher pound threatens competitiveness, trade levels and
the future balance of payments. It makes foreign prices appear
cheaper in terms of pounds which helps to control inflation. Overall
this affects the domestic economy as deflation, cutting spending,
growth, employment and inflation, but making British consumers
better off for the time being in terms of foreign goods and services.
Thus a rise in the exchange rate boosts the value of the pound in
your pocket, but makes it difficult for you to earn more pounds.

A fall in the exchange rate reverses all this. It helps competitiveness and reflates demand in the economy. It stimulates growth,
employment and inflation. It damages the value of the pound in
your pocket, especially when you try to spend abroad, or on goods
from abroad. But if exchange rate changes can be so significant and
contradictory in their effects on the economy, why are they allowed
to happen? Experience in the 1970s and 1980s showed dramatic and
disruptive changes, one way and then the other, on a number of
occasions (see Table 4.1). One problem is that the government is
limited in what it can do to change things. It can buy and sell from
the reserves, it can use taxes to affect spending on imports, and it can
influence interest rates to alter the flow of international money
deposits. But the scale of the market for pounds is now so huge that
it overwhelms much of what the government can offer. The govern-

TABLE 4.1
The Pound's Exchange Rate

Sterling exchange rate index (Av. 1985 = 1000)

1980	117.7
1981	119.0
1982	113.7
1983	105.3
1984	100.6
1985	100.0
1986	91.5
1987	90.1
1988	95.5
Mid-1989	91.1

SOURCE *Economic Trends* (London: HMSO, 1989)

ment also is constrained in its use of policy by other, domestic targets such as Budget balance and monetary growth.

Perhaps the main constraint in the 1980s was a belief that the government should not intervene too much. Free market forces would set the right exchange rate, if left to do so. Government policy would disguise and distort the signals, on inflation, interest rates and trading performance, that foreign exchange dealers use to decide the true balance of supply and demand. This may be true but is there a cost in finding out? Exchange rate fluctuations have been damaging, and the UK was alone in keeping out of the European Community's European Monetary System of stable exchange rates.

How to Play Markets, and Win

All of us are affected by markets including even those of the City. The money market sets interest rates which come through to house buyers with mortgages, and other types of loans. The foreign exchange market sets the value of the pound in exchange for foreign currencies and so influences trade, growth, jobs and inflation, and the value of the pound in your pocket. It is important to understand markets and to use them well and, if possible, to play them and win.

Speculation is when buyers and sellers deal in a market for short-term capital gain instead of out of genuine interest in whatever is being traded. Stock market speculators deal in shares not as an investment or from interest in the company but to gain from price changes from day to day. Property speculators buy and sell houses not because they really wish to live or work there but because they hope to profit from a rise in price. Foreign exchange speculators buy and sell currencies not because they need them to buy goods and services but to gain from expected changes in exchange rates between one deal and the next.

Expectations are crucial to all this activity. Any speculation is based on an expectation of future prices that compares favourably with the present price. But prices can go down as well as up and there is never any certainty that even the most likely of expectations will come about. If it does then speculators gain on their deal, but if it does not they lose instead. That is the risk they all face and their profit, if they make one, is a reward for their work as risk-takers. But some risks are greater than others. The successful speculator reads the signals of market behaviour carefully, relies on experience of market forces and the basic principles of supply and demand to predict the performance of price.

Consider the foreign exchange market, for instance. Good trade figures are likely to raise the exchange rate. The economic theory behind this is straightforward: greater demand for British goods implies greater demand for British currency with which to buy them. If a speculator can anticipate this happening he can buy pounds now at a relatively low price. When, and if the trade figures are announced to be encouraging then others will buy pounds as well, so pushing up market price. The speculator can then sell his unwanted pounds at their higher price and take the capital gain between the two transactions as profit.

Notice that one dealer on his own is such a small part of the market that he cannot affect it. It is when all participants act together in response to some common factor that market forces change price. A speculator gains most when he accurately leads those market forces, but if all speculators think and act together their expectation becomes self-fulfilling: by expecting price to rise, and buying to make a profit, they collectively cause it to rise. This explains why speculation can distort market price, aiming to anticipate changes but through this pack instinct actually exaggerating changes. Price fluctuates much higher and lower than it should go and no individual dealer has the influence to reverse the general expectation, and steady things down.

Speculators can profit from a capital gain from price changes. But they can do much better still because of the dealing time allowed in many markets. Consider stocks and shares. Deals to buy and sell shares are made all the time but settled, with an exchange of cash for certificates, only at intervals of a couple of weeks. In the meantime, therefore, it is possible to sell shares one does not yet own or offer to buy with cash one has not yet received. If all goes well the speculator will balance this deal with another later on, to buy the shares cheaper or to sell more expensively. Both deals will be settled at the same time leaving the speculator with a profit, for no initial outlay, but at greatly increased risk.

A similar approach is possible in other City markets: buying and selling forward rather than on the spot. Speculators can buy cocoa, say, for delivery and payment in several months time in the hope that sales prices will have risen by then. They can deal in currencies as bonds for settlement in three or six months time, by when they hope for an improved exchange rate. But this can be risky business. Who are the gamblers who live from such frequent speculation? Some are individuals who specialise in playing the markets, although they must have credibility with their brokers who act on their behalf that losses can be covered and debts paid. Most, however, are the ordinary trading and dealing companies already involved in their respective market. Cocoa futures are bought by cocoa companies as a hedge against future market changes and to secure supplies. Currencies are bought by the bankers of trading companies.

Chaos and Confusion

Some speculators base their expectations on expert, analytical comment by economists and other commentators, while some observe supply and demand forces on their own terms. Others are just as successful in some areas, however, by ignoring market forces altogether and instead observing statistical patterns and trends, or relying on hunch and intuition. Keynes made a fortune for himself and for his college, King's Cambridge, by playing the markets of the City but many economists do not enjoy the same success. Most are, after all, in research or teaching or writing rather than out in the City making their fortune. How is it that markets can reward apparently random, arbitrary interpretations?

Market behaviour is not always as systematic and predictable as simple economic principles would suggest. Rational economic decisions must be based on perfect information, and this is frequently absent from the real world. Investors read company reports and technical analysis but do not know if managers are running companies as efficiently as possible, or how competitors are preparing new products. International markets are influenced by world events, by political action and by war. Commodity markets depend on weather conditions to set the supply of primary products. In the face of such chaos and confusion, it can be misleading to predict future changes on the basis of past principles.

The general lack of knowledge in many markets can give speculators their best opportunity. Early or privileged information, given as a tip off or played as a hunch, can anticipate a predictable, general market trend. But insider dealing, where people trade on the basis of secret information that they should not disclose, is a fraud on the rest of the market and illegal. Nevertheless, it is true that many major take-overs that boost share prices because of extra buying to acquire a majority of shares are anticipated in the market. The share price starts to rise before any official announcement as people 'in the know' speculate for a quick, certain, illegal profit. Notice also that the rise in demand in itself informs others in the market of what may be afoot.

Markets may work somewhat imperfectly, therefore, in that prices fluctuate too high or too low from time to time. The lack of knowledge on the part of market traders can mislead them and disrupt other sections of the economy. In general, however, market forces fulfil a remarkable and valuable job. They match a host of individual intentions, decided by different people with different points of view. They unite all those people in one system but allow them individual freedom and personal sovereignty. They control the allocation of scarce resources to satisfy consumer wants as efficiently as possible, throughout the economy as a whole. Even market-makers and speculators perform a valuable part in all this for they make each market exceptionally sensitive and responsive to changing conditions. Such are the advantages of the free market system.

The Free Market System

The free market system allocates scarce resources between infinite consumer wants to satisfy, in ideal conditions, the greatest possible number. It relies upon the free and individual decisions of buyers and sellers of each factor of production and each good and service to determine how resources should be used and who should receive how much. There are markets for shares, housing and currencies, but also for bread, water, nurses, lawyers and everything else that people wish to exchange. The details of each market may differ greatly but the general principles of supply and demand, and how they set price and output do not.

Supply to each market is based on the employment of resources. More supply comes if producers hire more labour, more of all factors, at a cost in order to raise planned output. Demand is based upon consumers' satisfaction of their wants. Higher demand follows from greater income or a preference in favour of the good so that consumers are willing to pay relatively more for it. If wants change, say because environmental awareness leads people to put catalytic converters on their cars, this affects demand, supply and the allocation of resources.

The preference for 'clean' cars changes demand so that consumers are willing to pay more for converted cars but less for other things, and especially unconverted cars. Demand rises so increasing market price and output of converted cars. The higher price induces manufacturers to produce more of the converted cars instead of other types, and to achieve this they increase employment of labour, machinery and other factors in the new field. Entrepreneurs set up new companies to supply converters. Old-fashioned companies lose business and close down or transfer. Resources are re-employed in the new form of production due solely to the change in consumer tastes. Even shares will reflect this change as profits, share prices and investment rise in the new 'green' fields of industry.

Why go to all this trouble when the government might just have easily imposed the change as environmental reform? Advocates of the market system point out that no one expresses people's wants and priorities as well as they do themselves – through their individual decisions to buy different products. Furthermore, changes in one area of the economy are going to involve far-reaching compensations in all others, as achieved automatically through the invisible hand of the price mechanism. The change in demand for one product such as catalytic converters, for example, is only the start of the process that leads to new patterns of employment and investment in industry.

Mainly, however, the appeal of this system lies in its political and social implications as much as its economic efficiency. Individual choices to buy and sell, to consume and produce afford people the opportunity, indeed force upon them the compunction to decide their own fate. They enjoy freedom to buy what they want, and to work where and how they wish. But this motivates them to gain all the satisfaction they can from their income and all the income they can from their work. The free market system relies on avarice for its motive force, but offers economic efficiency and personal autonomy in return. It is not surprising to find, as in the next chapter, that there are different opinions on when and where to accept that deal.

To Regulate or Deregulate?

5

Privatisation has done wonders for the advertising industry and for merchant banking. It has achieved some of the largest ever company share flotations, as with the sale of British Gas to 4.5 million shareholders for £7750 million. It has established a number of national companies in the private rather than the public, state owned sector of industry. What may be its most durable effect, however, is to convert a generation of small savers to the habits of share ownership. People who previously would have been content for the government to be responsible for the conduct of essential public utilities found that they could easily claim a share of the action. Most of the nation's customers could not afford to or did not choose to buy shares, but those who did gained ownership of important companies at terms significantly below the eventual market price. Margaret Thatcher's dream of a nation with more shareholders than trade unionists moved that much closer.

Most questions of economic policy divide down two well-worn paths: whether to have central intervention or free enterprise, whether to assert collective or individual points of view, whether to favour a left-wing or right-wing approach. The post-war years heralded in an age of direct government controls to correct problems that had become all too apparent. Power, communications and transport were too important and too far gone in terms of disorganisation and inefficiency, it was felt, for the government to stand aside and watch. State ownership and control, through nationalisation of major industries and regulation of some others, brought an opportunity to overcome deep-seated problems. Some even saw it as a solution in its own right through changed attitudes and motivation.

The 1980s saw a change of heart, largely with a change of political leadership. But privatisation began as a specific opportunity to sell some shares in one or two firms, BP in particular, rather than as a general political principle. The sale raised billions of pounds, and helped to finance all-important cuts to government borrowing and taxation, at least for a while. Then came the brainwave: why not sell shares in other major, profitable public sector corporations to continue the budget benefits? As long as the stock market remained buoyant and welcomed the new issues the government would raise around £5 billion a year, which would be enough to take 3 or 4p off the standard rate of income tax. The ensuing record of the privatisation policy is illustrated in Table 5.1.

Financial expediency fortunately coincided with political principle. The government's support was for free enterprise, individualist, right-wing policies. Their belief was that production should be organised and owned by private shareholders to ensure efficient cost-minimisation and competitive profit-maximisation. The problem was to persuade potential shareholders that these companies – from British Telecom and British Airways through to British Coal and British Rail – were worth buying. Good advertising worked wonders here, at least in attracting interest in an entirely new way from the general public. But knowledgeable investors were interested in projected growth and profitability and the details of an official prospectus. This needed to reassure them on two points in particular.

One was the accumulated debt and running costs of the corporations, built up over many years of public sector price restraint, restricted investment, and inefficient working practices. Radical moves were needed to fatten some pigs for market. Old debts were written off, paid by the government. Tough management was introduced, in cars, steel and coal in particular, to cut unprofitable plants and poorly productive workforces, in some cases by half. Substantial price rises were allowed, indeed encouraged in some industries to meet the government's targets of profitability. The strategy was all going so well until the stock market crash of October 1988 ushered in a new era of more cautious investment, and discouraged further substantial new issues.

The other vital concern for both potential shareholders and

TABLE 5.1
UK Privatisation

Company	Date of sale	Percent sold[a] (%)	Gross Proceeds		
			Company £m	Government £m	Total £m
Amersham Int'l	February 1982	100	6	65	71
Associated	February 1983	51.5	56	(34)	22
British Ports	April 1984	48.5		52	52
BAA	July 1987	100		1281	1281
British	February 1981	51.6	100	50	150
Aerospace	May 1985	59	188	363	551
British Airways	February 1987	100		900	900
British Gas	December 1986	97[c]	(2286)	7720	5434
British	June 1977	17		564	564
Petroleum	November 1979	5		290	290
	September 1983	7		566	566
	October 1987	36.8	1515	5725	7240
British Telecom	November 1984	50.2	1290	2626	3916
Britoil	November 1982	51	–	549	549
	August 1985	48	–	449	449
Cable &	October 1981	49[d]	35	189	224
Wireless	December 1983	22	–	275	275
	December 1985	31	331	602	933
Enterprise Oil	June 1984	100		392	392
Jaguar[b]	July 1984	99		294	294
Rolls Royce	May 1987	100	283	1080	1363
	Total		1518	23 998	25 516

(a) May total more than 100% due to rights issues or less than 100% due to shares retained for loyalty bonus of employees.
(b) Proceeds to the Rover Group (then known as British Leyland); indirectly to HM Treasury via a lower public sector borrowing requirement for Rover.
(c) Sufficient shares retained to satisfy loyalty bonus arrangements
(d) A further 1% went directly to the Employee Share Ownership Plan.
SOURCE *Privatisation: The Facts* (London: Price Waterhouse, 1987).

customers is the market position of these firms. As nationalised utilities they virtually all enjoyed a state-imposed monopoly. Only British Telecom could sell telephone communications and equipment, only British Airways could fly certain routes, only British Gas could produce and supply piped gas. Free and open competition would require an end to these practices and so there were concessions, to Merlin telecommunications, on sales of telephones and to other air operators, for example. But it was essential for the future profitability of the companies that shareholders should see their position of monopoly to be fundamentally secure. Monopolies are a good investment.

The Danger of Dominance

Why does it matter if firms grow to dominate their markets? Monopoly is the situation where a single firm is the only seller in its market, as the Water Boards are each the only providers of piped water and mains drainage in their areas. More common are the forms of imperfect competition such as oligopoly, where just a few firms share market supply, or duopoly, where there are two firms only. Monopolistic competition is a special case where there are many otherwise perfectly competitive firms each separating off its own part of the market through product differentiation, advertising and customer allegiance. In all these situations the firm has some power to influence market price by adjusting its output. It is this monopoly power that is considered so important by shareholders and managers, but potentially threatening to customers.

Economists identify this threat most clearly by comparing identical markets supplied by perfectly competitive and monopoly firms. Under perfect competition firms sell only by price. Consumers are free to choose the cheapest of the identical products sold by many, many firms. All firms' prices and costs are brought as low as possible, therefore, to ensure a reasonable level of profits, but totally efficient production and the best possible service to the customer. All this represents an ideal though unlikely situation but is often interpreted as a target to be aimed for. Thus competition should be encouraged not just for the benefit of a particular band of consumers, but in the wider public interest for the best possible use of the nation's resources.

Monopoly is different, and perhaps very different, as shown in Figure 5.1. The single firm has power to sell whatever and however it wishes to its market. It may use this power in the public interest, but a privately owned monopoly is more likely to be concerned with its shareholders' profits. Profit maximisation is served by restricting output below competitive levels in order to cut total costs and raise price. Some customers are turned away by the higher price, and if there were significant competition this retreat would damage sales and market share. As it is, with no close alternatives available, customers must either pay up or do without. They lose out either way but the monopoly makes greater profits from less work. It uses economic resources less efficiently, and the attraction of this power will encourage it to maintain barriers against competition.

Without any barriers it would be possible for new firms to set up in competition for a monopolist's profits and market share. But managers want to secure their jobs and shareholders to protect their profits. Thus the incentive to obstruct potential competitors is even

FIGURE 5.1
Market Dominance

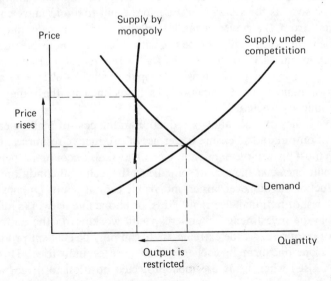

greater than that to maximise profits. What can be done? One approach is to keep a high price, high selling costs policy through non-price aspects of marketing. New and better products, brand names, advertising, and control of distribution outlets all help win customer allegiance, and discourage new competitors. Economies of scale and accumulated profits also allow dominant firms to undercut competitors at a loss, until they close down, to re-establish market power. Best of all, however, is to have market power that is based on legal authority, from patent rights or as a state maintained monopoly such as the nationalised, now privatised public corporations.

Policy for Monopoly

Luckily, considering the number and significance of firms with monopoly power in the economy, the argument is not as one-sided as that. Monopoly power can be strong or weak depending on consumers' preferences for the product. Thus public utilities such as power, transport and communications are vitally important in general but allow for choices between gas or electricity, plane or rail or bus, post or phone to maintain a measure of competition between them. Companies may be run for reasons other than to maximise profits, such as for security in the market and to avoid unwelcome interest from the government, competitors or corporate raiders. Public utilities especially will be run with efficient, responsible public service in mind. Most important of all is the question of efficiency from very large, capital intensive companies such as electricity and telecommunications. Competition in fields such as these may be economically wasteful.

Economies of scale allow a reduction in the cost of making each unit of output and so ensure better use of productive resources. But firms must grow large enough to gain all available economies before this efficiency is achieved. In some fields the technical conditions of production favour ever larger, indivisible capital plant. Duplicated rail lines, or national electricity grids, or phone line networks inflict double the investment for undercapacity working on the nation's scarce resources. At the extreme, there can only be efficient production from one firm in each of these sorts of industries. This is emphasised when firms use their protected position to invent and develop new products and processes. Monopolies are often the bravest innovators. It is an irony that the more they are equipped to do this, however, the less competitive motivation they have to actually do so.

How should the government treat monopoly power? Clearly there is a need for caution, and for information about behaviour that threatens the public interest. The Office of Fair Trading performs this function for the government in Britain, although the development of European trade and the single market make the European Community agencies for competition policy possibly more important. Action in restraint of free competition on the part of producers is banned by law, in most cases. Mergers to create dominant monopolies are subject to possible investigation, delay or prevention, as seen in Chapter 3. That leaves monopoly, which can be investigated if thought to be acting against the public interest. But each case is taken on its own merits because of the complicated balance that can result from monopoly exploitation of markets on the one hand, and efficient production and development work on the other.

Where does this lead the argument on privatisation? Public utilities are especially significant for the strength and scale of their monopoly power but can justify it on grounds of national efficiency. The question becomes one of ensuring good behaviour, therefore, and this can warrant study by the Monopolies Commission whether the firms are owned privately or by the state. Nationalisation might ensure more complete control of the company's aims and objectives, but seems to threaten efficiency. Privatised firms could be controlled in other ways, and recent experience suggests what these are.

Shares were offered to customers at preferential terms, and the government laid down in the companies' charters their obligations towards their customers. OFTEL was set up to monitor consumer satisfaction, complaints and compliance with that charter by Telecom. Thus public sector supervision of privatised monopolies is still possible. There have been criticisms, however, that these watchdogs lack teeth, and that a genuine priority for competitive efficiency would have led to the sale of separated, competitive companies. That would have cut the government's privatisation receipts, but it might well also have harmed the efficiency potential of the large, natural monopolies involved.

No Privacy These Days

Public utilities such as the power, communications and transport industries are often described as having a responsibility beyond that to their shareholders and customers alone. These are private issues, based on what economists describe as private costs and benefits. The price BR charges its customer is the private cost to him of taking the train journey. The customer decides that this is a cost worth paying by comparing it with the benefit gained, from the pleasure of seeing people or the value of getting work done, which measures private benefit. And the price that BR charges covers the cost of producing the product by employing resources such as machinery and workers: this is the private cost of production.

Public values, however, take in wider considerations. There may be spin-offs that affect other producers, the use of other resources, the satisfaction felt by other consumers. Social benefit, as it is called in economics, measures these wider benefits to the rest of society as well as to the private individual involved in any act of consumption. Many activities will have no wider benefits to speak of, but rail travellers may keep isolated communities in touch, may maintain business and employment, or may reduce congestion on the roads. Social cost includes wider disadvantages, again to those not directly involved in a purchase. There may be noise, dirt or danger to others. There may be inconvenience and congestion.

The nationalised/privatised sector of industry typically produces a significant array of these secondary effects on society, through social costs and benefits. These reflect the social significance of key areas of national production. In purely economic terms, they identify the 'commanding heights of the economy' that attracted most political attention in Labour's nationalisation programme. Power industries such as coal, gas, nuclear and electricity are essential for the production of all other manufactures and services. They are essential for domestic services in the home. But they are also at the frontier of environmental protection on issues such as nuclear waste, open cast mining and power station emissions. Transport and communications are another part of the productive infrastructure of the economy responsible for the location, patterns and quality of modern life. Issues such as green belt building, road safety and congestion and up-to-date information technology depend on the policies and performance of the road, rail, bus, postal and telecommunications industries.

Transport policy is one example, however, that leads on to countless grey areas emerging from black and white distinctions of private from social effects. Traffic congestion impedes the efficiency of production in society as a whole, but is also an individual inconvenience that many will pay to overcome, through intercity rail journeys, say, or commercial motorway links. Roads may offer a general social benefit and be provided on that basis but the Severn Bridge, Channel Tunnel and other projects run commercially, or even privately. Can private and public values be separated? If so, why should some forms of transport such as roads be offered only by the state, free to users, while others such as rail are expected to operate on a commercial (albeit loss-making) basis? A similar confusion seems to apply to basic manufacturing industries such as cars, steel and shipbuilding. These have all been nationalised for their significance to the economy at large, but privatised as competing, commercial industries. Did they have a social role, and do they fulfil it still?

Allowing for the Unaccountable

The division between private and social values leaves a great deal of room for interpretation. As so often in what are initially economic matters this involves political judgement. Economics is concerned with objective alternatives, but the politicians must choose between them on the basis of policy targets and subjective values. There is one point, however, that objective economics leads us to. Economic efficiency involves the use of scarce resources to satisfy the greatest number of economic wants, but the presence of external costs and benefits makes this possible only through some process of collective accounting and decision-making. Social effects can only be measured, can only be allowed for by government.

The very nature of social costs and benefits means that they happen as indirect results of other individuals' decisions, and are not measured directly as prices in the market place. They can be difficult to identify, difficult even to measure accurately. They are easily dismissed or disregarded, especially by the firms directly involved.

Thus it was with issues of pollution and environmental protection, raised in the context of Third World development, in Chapter 1. The person who commits pollution by discharging waste does so for free, knowing that the cost of cleaning up, if it is done at all, will be borne by someone else, possibly far away. Those whose environment suffers from acid rain cannot find out who is directly responsible for it, nor charge them for it.

National governments can take account of social costs and social benefits that are caused and felt by their own citizens, provided these can be identified, measured and compensated for in some way. Extreme cases of pollution may damage health or the environment in an irreversible way, or a way that is unattributable to its perpetrators. Dangerous industrial wastes may be buried inadequately and reappear generations later. Nuclear wastes may remain deadly some centuries after those who created them have themselves died. The owners of Three Mile Island nuclear power station at first described the accident there as 'a normal aberration'. But normal aberrations can be cured and charged for. The problem of accountability and enforcement is even worse in international matters. The interdependence of world production and of world ecology requires an equivalent route between peoples in different countries, which is not yet present. The greenhouse effect is a shared problem. Without a shared solution it could yet become irreversible.

There may once have been a time when the nature of technical production and the nature of government itself made this less of a problem. The medieval world suffered its own problems: plague, fire and lawlessness might all be described, with a little licence, as economic social costs. The form of government clarified social values, since any personal cost to the sovereign was interpreted as a cost to society. Modern systems of government allow for more sophisticated, and one would hope more accurate methods of assessment. It is difficult to conceive of a way to make individuals feel direct responsibility for their economic actions, however. The world's religions aim for a moral code, communism aims for dedication only to the collective good. But do these overcome individual ignorance of the effects of one's actions, and selfish disregard for the costs to others?

Do As You Would Be Done By

How can the government help the economy take account of social costs and benefits? Suppose there is some pollution, for example, from the dumping of chemical waste on an unsuitable site from which poisons enter the water system. One approach aims to use economic decision-making, indeed the same sort of decision-making that led the polluting firm to choose to discharge on the site in the first place: because this was the lowest cost, highest profit solution to their individual disposal problem. The difference that the government would introduce would be to charge the company the full cost of their decision. The principle is that the polluter should pay to clean up their own pollution.

There would be a number of elements to this, if it were to work successfully. First, the government would have to assess the nature and extent of the costs borne by the rest of society. These would include the cost of cleaning the water supply and redumping the waste in a safe form, at a safe place. They would extend further, however, to the hardship suffered by those consuming the water or observing the damaged environment. This would require satisfactory compensation. Altogether these costs would be charged to the polluter to allow the government to afford the cleaning up process.

Of course, those who had suffered would much prefer that such pollution should not happen at all. The advantage of this approach, once it is working systematically and effectively, is that firms are deterred commercially from the decisions that lead to pollution. The choice between alternatives that were originally costed only in private terms now has social effects costed and built in to the decision as well. If pollution happens anyway it is because that is still the cheapest way for the company to behave, as a representative of society as a whole. It is much more likely, however, that the firm will now choose a cleaner method of working, and so achieve a more efficient use of society's resources.

How might this work more generally? Every social cost would need to be identified, attributed and costed accurately, and then charged as a tax on the perpetrator (Figure 5.2). There should be a tax on noisy parties, on dogs fouling the park, or on leaving litter. By contrast every social benefit should be encouraged economically through a subsidy from the government, set to reflect the degree of advantage offered. There should be subsidies paid to those who stay

FIGURE 5.2
A Tax on Social Costs

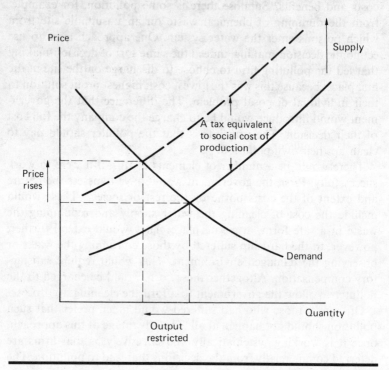

off congested, rush hour roads, to good neighbours and good citizens. This is a fine approach, of course, and extends individual decision-making to the arena of social as well as private effects. But can it work? It seems doubtful, especially in cases where social effects can neither be measured or attributed accurately. If polluters believe they can get away with it, even while others face a realistic charge for what they do, the pollution will continue.

The Surgical Approach

Some social costs are too severe to even be considered for this tax/subsidy treatment. Certain individual actions are irreversible, so that an initial social cost grows and grows without limit. The spread of a contagious and deadly disease is like this: there is no room to allow sick individuals to decide if they would prefer subsidised treatment, they must be confined for everyone else's protection. High-level nuclear waste offers something of the same threat, in that the first accident could be the last. Similarly, with other threats to life it would be wrong to let the damage happen at all, whatever the ensuing compensation.

Some social costs result from irrational economic behaviour because of flaws in the decision-making process. There is less point in taxing drugs, cigarettes or alcohol to discourage their unsocial effects if consumers' addiction or intoxication confuses their rational response. Drunken drivers are a menace because the first effect of their drinking is to give them bad judgement – of their ability, their drunkenness, and driving conditions. They certainly could not judge the significance or importance of a tax in these circumstances. Addicts deny themselves any choice at all by their physical dependence.

What of international phenomena such as the greenhouse effect, acid rain or even terrorism? These cannot often be attributed to individuals, or even individual national governments. No individual or market based deterrent could be devised to reverse such processes as the erosion of the tropical rain forests. It needs agreed international cooperation to further the mutual self-interest of all on the planet. Such agreement requires a substantial degree of both imagination and trust, and initiative such as has rarely been enjoyed in international diplomacy. Even then it requires something more: enforcement.

Governments within each country face the same problem over and over again. How are individuals to be guided to take account of social values, of the effect of their actions on others, when they cannot directly be faced with what they have done? It is not possible to tax every noisy party, every dirty dog or every litter lout, because they cannot be caught. It is at this point that law takes over from economics. Instead of taxes society uses fines. Instead of subsidies it offers rewards, and honours. Unsocial activity is banned rather than costed and relative values are reflected in the degree of the offence. Thus society uses government decree and regulation to enforce, in some measure at least, on some people for some of the time, its recognition of social costs and benefits.

Benefits to Society

Taxes and regulations can treat unsocial actions that result in another person's dissatisfaction but it may be harder to regulate for positive social effects. The government cannot order everyone to show consideration and to perform good deeds, by decree, much though it might wish to. Social benefits may invite a different approach, therefore. We must ask how these benefits are linked with costs and to see how they lie at the heart of much economic analysis.

A consumer chooses to consume a good only for the satisfaction of wants that it offers, and it is the ability to satisfy a want that makes any product into a 'good' rather than a 'bad'. The positive satisfaction of wants are economic benefits, gained either privately by the consumer individually or publicly by others in society due to secondary, external effects. Whether an individual has to pay for these benefits or not is irrelevant to their value. Indeed, market conditions allow most consumers to buy goods for less than they are worth to them in terms of benefits. This bargain benefit is called a consumer surplus.

Costs, on the other hand, result from dissatisfaction, from wants failing to be met. These also can affect individual consumers directly, as when paying for a good to deprive one of possible satisfaction from spending on something else. There can also be external costs resulting from dissatisfaction to others not directly involved. In every case the cost results exactly from some benefit that is forgone, and is measured by the value of that lost benefit. If no benefits are lost there is no cost and the decision comes for free, in economic terms. Generally, we know that any economic cost is an opportunity cost, measured by the next best alternative forgone.

External benefits to others in society are like consumer surplus in that they are not paid for, but different in that the individual consumer has no motivation to consider them. Those who do receive these benefits do so for free and would act irrationally in offering to pay. One does not satisfy as many wants as possible by paying for what are offered as free rides. Thus social benefits are considered by neither the consumers who generate them nor the consumers who receive them. They may arise by accident but are more likely to be neglected and underprovided in the free market system. It is the role of government to arrange an adequate provision.

Merit Goods

Consider health and education. People are willing to pay for their education, or for the education of their children, for the satisfaction it gives them. It is seen as part of growing up, a good start in life, and it is interesting in its own right. Furthermore, it is an investment, perhaps the main investment anyone ever makes, in youngsters' abilities, experience and character. Thus education could be offered only privately, and sold to those who could afford it and appreciate its value. But this would not be enough. Education offers substantial social benefits as well. We all gain from having well-behaved, capable and productive people around us. The nation gains from improved resources and the humanity of its citizens. Thus the state should encourage further provision of education, as it does, for all children. The case might well be widened beyond that.

Health care is similar. People would pay to feel well, perhaps more willingly than for almost anything else. But it is in the interests of society as a whole, including the healthy people in it, to maintain an active, fit population. Contagious disease needs treatment on behalf of those who have not caught it, but might otherwise do so. Again the social benefits warrant government intervention to ensure that enough health care is available to all the people. Thus education and health care are examples of merit goods that offer substantial social as well as private benefits (Figure 5.3). But how should the government act to ensure the correct level of provision?

There are two main approaches that divide, as might be expected, along the familiar fault line between free enterprise and collective values. Supporters of free enterprise favour private provision of merit goods through private hospitals, private nursing, private schools, and so forth. The government's role would be limited to a necessary minimum, to purchase these facilities as seen fit in the interests of the social benefits of its citizens. This scheme retains the advantages of private production where efficiency and customer service is encouraged through profit maximisation. It conflicts with the priority of the alternative approach, however, which is to stress community interests and social values through public enterprise: state maintained hospitals and schools.

The trend in Britain, fostered for political reasons, has been towards contracting out, indeed privatising merit good production.

FIGURE 5.3
Provision of Merit Goods

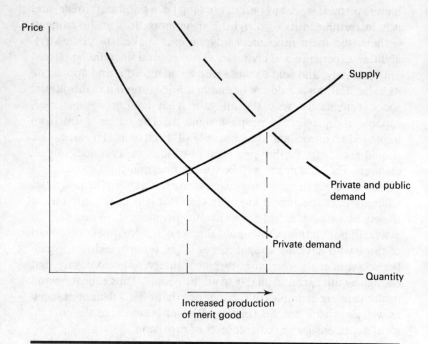

The state pays subsidies for production through schemes such as dental, optical and prescription charges, hospital pay beds, assisted places at private schools. Individual doctors, hospital administrators and headteachers and governors are given increased autonomy over their own spending and selling of services. Probably this does motivate these individuals to achieve a more efficient use of their resources, but does it offer as good a service to consumers in society? Social benefits are so difficult to identify and to measure that we will probably never know the full answer. Which should only encourage the argument!

Public Goods

The problem with merit goods is to ensure an adequate provision that reflects their benefits to society. The problem with certain other goods and services which also are of significant value to society is to ensure that any are provided at all. National defence, law and order, public rights of way, street lighting, lighthouses and shipping markers are all examples of public goods. These offer so many social benefits, so widely, that if just one person buys them then everyone else can gain the same benefits as well, on a free ride. However much one person buys, the benefits are shared so much that there is never less for any one else. But there is a catch, for if everyone expects to be able to claim a free ride no one will be motivated to take the initial step of buying the good. It would be an act of charity to others to do so and, with some of the examples above such as defence or national street lighting, an extremely expensive gesture into the bargain.

Public goods, therefore, must be provided collectively by society for the good of society, or not at all. In fact these products typically stand as illustrations of the first areas of economic responsibility ever performed by the state. Nowadays there is, again, a choice over the method of provision. It is still possible to produce through private firms even though the product is unsellable, provided the government levies taxes in order to pay a subsidy, in this case at 100 per cent of the costs. Alternatively, the government could set up production firms owned by the state, again financed from taxation, to produce through public enterprise.

Both ways require citizens collectively to pay their money but then they take their choice about the more efficient method of supply. In Britain these choices have led to some strange arrangements: the army is centrally funded and run, rights of way are protected by local authorities or National Parks or private charities such as the Ramblers Association. The emergency services of police, fire and ambulance are run locally but financed centrally, while the lifeboats are the leading private charity in the country.

A Case of Public Enterprise

What then is the case for public enterprise in what is essentially a private enterprise economy? We have seen that the argument is built up in a number stages, each subject to disagreement between free market and collectivist economists. One issue is the control of dominant firms in areas of vital public interest. Privatised companies may have their behaviour monitored in other ways, through regulation and interindustry competition, but public ownership may allow for more stringent control. It was interesting to observe in the sequence of excellent privatisation trailers advertising gas, phones, water and electricity one that particularly caught the eye: a billboard poster selling the British Army plc. In fact this was an advert for an all-powerful lager, but some people did not quite see the joke. Perhaps the armed forces would operate more efficiently as a privately owned concern. A charter and Office of Fair Trading in Armed Might (OFTAM) would protect the public interest adequately – wouldn't it?

Efficiency in production is not just a matter of motivation, of course. It depends also on the technical possibilities, and especially the scope for economies of scale. These are so significant in most of the national utilities that can be termed natural monopolies. Competition within each industry would waste scarce national resources. Nationalisation for many of the power, transport and communications industries came at a time when rationalisation and investment was needed to achieve this efficiency within a new, national framework.

Privatisation came at a different time when national monopolies would face strong international and interindustry competition, and when economies of scale had been achieved. It is not the argument about ownership that is so important for their development as that about investment. If government policy would restrict the flow of funds available to these industries through public borrowing, then they would indeed be more efficiently run in the private sector where their access to investment would be decided only on commercial criteria. It was expedient to nationalise many firms given the conditions of the time and the threat of closure, and it became equally expedient to relaunch them onto the private sector. Rolls-Royce, Rover cars, and Amersham International are not significantly different from their competitor companies except in that they have once been state owned.

The main argument over public enterprise, however, centres on public benefits and the social role of the particular industries involved. The 'commanding heights' of the economy have an influence on the performance of the economy and the efficiency of the national economy that goes beyond their mere size. They have a strategic significance in determining the allocation of national resources and the competitiveness of national industry. In one sense, this emphasises the responsibility for government patronage; in another, it highlights the need for fully efficient, low cost, highly reliable production.

Privatisation Rules

The trend towards deregulation in recent years has been founded on arguments of economic efficiency, but then built up and extended in other directions altogether. Political values have led the way in this and a leading feature across a range of government policies has been the encouragement of a property owning democracy. A fundamental distinction between left-wing socialists and right-wing Conservatives has traditionally been drawn on this question of ownership of the resources of production. Socialism starts with property owned by all the people collectively in order that it may be used to satisfy all their wants, collectively. Conservatives believe in *laissez-faire* capitalism where private individuals own the factors of production and use them to maximise their individual earnings. This is the motivation needed to ensure the efficiency of the free market system.

The government has encouraged share ownership through Personal Equity Plan tax concessions, and has encouraged the expansion of mortgage finance to allow home ownership. Most people's saving and investment has traditionally been in this area of home ownership, but also in institutional programmes such as life assurance and pensions. New tax arrangements here have discouraged life assurance but encouraged personal pension schemes so that people take a more active part in the investment of their savings in stocks and shares, for their future. Beyond all this, however, loom the programmes of privatisation and deregulation that have done so much to alter attitudes and behaviour in society.

Council house sales have proved a dramatic political success. This was a sector populated by traditional, working-class Labour supporters who tended to stay in their homes, renting from the local authority, sometimes for many, many years. The national government offered these residents the option of buying their homes at prices well below current market values. Those who chose to do so gained their greatest asset at a bargain price to live in, or sell off later at a profit. At a stroke, therefore, they gained a mortgage, a debt of gratitude to the Conservative government and membership of the property owning, capitalist classes. At the same time, the local authority, however unwillingly, raised funds to offset expenditure on new housing or other programmes. As a whole these property sales raised almost as much as the privatisation sales themselves.

Deregulation has allowed the introduction of competition into a range of traditionally protected, comfortable areas. Private sector companies have been allowed to set up closer rivals to state services: Mercury telecommunications, Sky satellite broadcasting, BUPA health insurance, and so forth. Public services have been hived off and contracted out to privately owned operators: local refuse collections, school catering and cleaning, and contracted bus operators, for example. Education has been reformed with a host of initiatives to encourage entrepreneurial attitudes, habits and skills in the young and vocational, market-based training. The universities and polytechnics face tough competition for funds to offer courses, employ staff and promote research. Sponsorship and commercially attractive attitudes and programmes have been encouraged in the arts and in sport.

On top of all this comes the flagship of privatisation: billion pound sales of famous corporations to attract attention throughout the world as well as at home; prices set to ensure a successful launch so that the number of bids for shares exceeds the number of shares on offer; prices high enough to raise substantial sums for the government budget, but not too high. It is important for the programme as a whole that each sale rewards its new shareholders with a market premium so that they can sell their new shares at a profit on the open market, if they so wish, the day after they bought them from the government. In a number of cases, of course, that speculative profit turned out to be quite extraordinary. Important also that the City be seen to attract all the investment it has guaranteed and not be left, as in the case of British Oil, with an embarrassing and costly shortfall. Thus a generation of customers, employees and first-time investors were attracted into share ownership as a new way of life. Not bad for a policy intended to help the government balance its books for a year or two!

A State of Envy

The government often has motives that are more complicated than they at first appear, even in purely economic terms. We can identify a range of arguments for and against public enterprise, we can comment on the range of issues associated with a programme of policies such as privatisation. And yet in all this there is still a dimension missing. That is the matter of what is yours and what is mine, what for the rich and what for the poor: the issue of income distribution.

The distribution of personal incomes describes this allocation between different individuals and groups in society. Every government takes a view and devises policies to affect distribution, although political judgements may overwhelm the economics. For economic efficiency it is enough that each person is rewarded according to the value of the work they put in to the economy. Subjective, political issues decree that the allocation be adjusted to favour particular groups, however. The Conservatives seek to reward the wealth creators who save, invest and take risks; or 'our people' more generally. Labour favour trade union members, workers and the underprivileged.

Behind these differences lies a surprisingly large area of agreement, however, that the state should protect its citizens and guarantee a minimum standard of living at least. Thus the Welfare State provides benefits from the cradle to the grave, but especially in relation to need at times of unemployment, poverty, ill health, childhood and old age. The same concern with social justice is reflected in eternal British values not so much of fair play as of support for the underdog. This Robin Hood principle of taking from the rich to give to the poor runs through the structure of taxation, at least in part, although again there have been pronounced and radical changes by recent Conservative governments. Recent Budgets have made the tax system roughly proportional in its impact on low, middle and high incomes; only very low earners and very high earners are taxed proportionately less.

But do public enterprise and privatisation policies reflect similar sympathies towards a preferred income distribution? In effect they do. Nationalised industries adopt pricing policies that favour some groups of customers through cross-subsidisation by others. Inter-

City rail routes, for example, balance some of the losses of London commuter services, and highly productive coal pits in Nottinghamshire offset the losses of some in other areas. Public asset sales have offered an advantage in terms of capital gain to council house buyers and share buyers.

Thus the government is a leading player in the national distribution game, and the ball used on the roulette table of advantage and disadvantage is envy. If the red side wins then the private propertied classes are left to cast longing looks on the state-owned assets of housing and public enterprise. If the blue side wins the distribution of gains is changed and workers are left to look enviously on the shares, houses and other properties sold off by the state to private owners. The state's weapons of regulation and deregulation, public enterprise and privatisation tip the balance of advantage one way or the other.

The
Money-go-round

6

'Let us unite to win the battle against inflation.' This was the rallying call to arms that dominated so much of government economic policy in the 1980s. Inflation was the enemy, the cause of other economic problems, the threat that would undermine the values and stability of the economic system. But what is it about inflation that prompts such anger and attention, and has it really deserved this reputation as economic public enemy number one?

The first feature of inflation, and one that explains much of its notoriety, is that it can be readily identified. Many economic issues are complicated and confused and change from one time to another. The picture of the bandit pinned up on the wanted poster needs to be clearly and easily remembered: preferably with a black patch, a scar and red beard. Inflation comes as close as any economic variable does to this sort of familiarity. Inflation is a rise in the general level of prices, so that all goods and services and paid work cost more in terms of pounds. Conversely, each pound buys less in terms of goods, services and work. This is usually measured in the cost of living index, the index of retail prices, that is announced by the government each month. Thus one line on the news headlines each month is all it takes to describe the rise or fall of inflation.

Everyone meets inflation in their spending and earning, hears of inflation in economic commentaries and government statements, and understands inflation at least in terms of the simple measure of its level over the month, or over the year. That level has changed immoderately over the years as shown in Table 6.1. Expressed as an

TABLE 6.1
UK Inflation

Percentage rise in the general index of retail prices	
1980	18.0
1981	11.9
1982	8.6
1983	4.6
1984	5.0
1985	6.1
1986	3.4
1987	4.2
1988	4.9
Mid-1989	8.2

SOURCE   *Economic Trends* (London: HMSO, 1989).

average rise in prices over a year as a whole, inflation has always
been present but as high as 18 per cent in 1980 and as low as 3 per
cent in 1986. Over a period of years there is something of a cycle as
high values are followed by low ones. But also there has been a long-
term deterioration from decade to decade as inflation tended to rise
from the 1950s to the 1960s to the 1970s. It was then, with values up
to 20 per cent and 30 per cent a year and a threat of runaway,
hyperinflation up to South American levels that inflation gained its
status in the UK as economic enemy number one. We would prefer
to keep inflation down to Japan's level (0.1 per cent in 1987) than up
to Bolivia's (8000 per cent in 1985).

Why Does Inflation Matter?

It may be a relatively simple matter to read the measure of inflation
but from then on things become much more complicated. People's
view of inflation and why it matters becomes confused with a host of
other and different issues in economics. They see inflation to be high
and rising, and understand that at least, but then see that unemploy-

ment is bad as well, that economic growth is down, strikes and taxes up, and the balance of payments in decline. They assume that these economic trends are connected, as they may be, and that inflation has caused all the trouble, which it has not. Inflation is not the cause of all evil in economics, but only specific results, and even then only under specific circumstances.

Inflation is a general rise in prices, but only within the national economy itself. Other countries may have more or less inflation so that their producers' prices are becoming less or more competitive than ours. So what matters for the balance of payments and international exchange rate of the pound is UK inflation relative to competitor countries. Relatively high inflation is damaging to the UK's international position, and over the years inflation has indeed been relatively high here. Even when inflation was falling fastest in the 1980s it was still higher than the European average, for example, in all but one year.

Inflation is a general rise in prices, but only for those prices that are free to move. People often feel that this works to their disadvantage, but they are confused. They see prices rising as they go shopping, for example, but take less notice of the same inflationary increase in their annual salary. Over the economy as a whole, on average, wages and other incomes from work rise just as much as prices since that is what inflation means. But those with particular types of incomes, or paying particular types of prices, may indeed move ahead or behind others. Some payments are fixed and do not adjust to inflation. Some trade unions keep their members' incomes up with or ahead of inflation better than others.

Consider loans at fixed interest rates, for instance. Most long-term borrowing is of this type, not by private households on mortgages, of course, but as loans to the government or to companies through long-term securities. These borrowers gain at times of inflation and the government, with its National Debt representing the largest in the country, stands to gain most. But if they gain someone else must be losing, and the individuals who see the value of their savings in long-term stocks erode through inflation include all current and future pensioners. Thus inflation allows the government and other debtors to gain at the expense of their creditors. This encourages spending and borrowing but discourages lending, at fixed rates at least. The old adage becomes 'not a lender but a borrower be'.

Inflation that can be anticipated is not much of a problem.

Perhaps the most damaging result follows from unanticipated inflation, however, in undermining the basis of the economy. Modern economics is based on exchange, of work for products, of one specialism for another, and that exchange process relies on money. If people lose their trust in money they will refuse to accept it, stop using it, and wreck the exchange process that is essential for advanced living standards. Those who most angrily oppose inflation do so in the belief that it tends naturally to accelerate, to undermine the basis of money confidence, and so to threaten the roots of our society. But surely people's confidence in money is not so fragile as this would suggest? We must answer that by observing what money is and where it comes from.

Where Money Comes From

Happiness may be made in heaven but money is made on earth. It is a man-made invention and its form, value and use is entirely a matter of convenience. Anything that people choose to use as money serves as money and is generally acceptable in the settlement of debt. We grow up with notes and coin as the most common, basic medium of exchange, but discover later that bank accounts are much more significant. Only around £1 of every £10 spent as money these days takes physical form as currency; the rest is exchanged through cheques or other banking arrangements. Really, no physical presence is needed at all except to confirm and maintain people's trust in the medium of money. Thus money is a true 'con trick', based entirely and only on people's confidence in it. It must be the largest and most successful con trick of all time.

Most money comes from banks and is kept in banks. To understand the nature of money and the causes of inflation, therefore, it is necessary to understand the work of banks, especially high street banks such as Barclays and Lloyds. Some of this work involves giving advice to customers and offering a range of services in the role of 'general practitioner' of personal finance. Some involves keeping customers' funds safe, in the same way as jewellery and deeds can be kept safe in the banks' safety deposit boxes. What is more interesting, however, is the way banks act as productive firms in the monetary sphere by putting customers' deposits to work for them, and more especially for the bank itself. Suppose you have £100 in your bank account so that you can write cheques up to that amount. Does this mean that you could find all your money sitting at your local branch, waiting for you to collect it as notes and coin? It may be better not to think too closely about this for the answer is probably no.

Banks have learnt over the years that very little of their customers' deposits will be withdrawn at any one time. A small percentage of total deposits, perhaps around 10 per cent, is all they need to keep available as cash or other reserves. The larger the bank, the more consistent this proportion will become. The more secure the bank and its type of business, the lower this proportion will become. But what about all the rest? Clearly, it is to the benefit of both the bank and its customers if that can be put to work, as capital, lent out at a rate of interest. Most of your deposits, therefore, will have been lent to other customers of the bank, for a given period of time at a given rate of interest. Your withdrawal can be paid for only because other customers do not wish to withdraw all their funds at the same time. If they did, because of lost confidence and a run on the bank, it would become technically bankrupt.

All banks put their funds to work in this way. Loan customers are willing to pay a rate of interest in order to have money available to invest in their business or buy goods and services. But notice what happens as they borrow and spend in this way: the money is redeposited in another bank account and subjected again to the same reserve/loans procedure. An initial bank deposit, from your money, say, generates a succession of further loans and deposits. And each of these deposits serves as money, being generally acceptable in exchange, in its own right. It is no wonder that most money takes the form of bank accounts rather than notes and coin. This is the way in which banks make money both for the economy to use and for their shareholders to enjoy as profit.

Cash, Loans and Interest Rates

Money represents immediate purchasing power, or liquidity as it is called, and can be transformed into goods and services through exchange. When the bank uses your money to make loans to customers, however, those loans are not liquid. A loan for one month does not get paid back as liquid cash until the end of that period of time. Loans for different periods of time, or at differing risk that they may not be repaid, represent different exchanges of liquidity. The price of each exchange is measured by the rate of interest agreed on the loan. Longer or riskier loans command a higher rate of interest.

The door to banking success is now open. Every banker wants to borrow funds at a low rate of interest in order to lend again at a higher rate of interest. The market is as close to perfect competition as it is possible to find so banks must follow general principles. They must work for their money but, in essence, they borrow short term in order to lend long, or at greater risk. The work involved is in the arrangement of several debts in order to finance each loan out to a customer and in taking the risk of being left bankrupt if debts rise or customers fail to repay.

Money and interest rates are thus connected in the same way as any commodity and its price. An increase in the supply of money, due, for instance, to improved arrangements for bank lending, increases the quantity lent and cuts the price charged – which is the rate of interest. Each length and type of loan may have its own market conditions and rate of interest, but the general level of rates for all can change. A rise in interest rates, by contrast, will encourage banks to lend more and customers to borrow less. Banks are likely to be already limited by what is their safe reserve/loans ratio. Companies will have to cut back on stocks, production and investment projects due to be financed by borrowing, however, and private households will cut back on hire purchase, consumer and other credit. High interest rates limit the demand for borrowing, new bank lending and the growth of bank deposits. Thus high interest rates cut the growth of the money supply.

The Value of Money

Money is a man-made invention and exists only in the mind: if people think that something represents purchasing power then, sure enough, it does. Thus money has no value in itself. Your notes and coin are good for nothing except ornamentation or ballast, and you may as well throw the lot away – but for the convention that they can be exchanged with other people for goods and services. Anyone who hoards coin for itself is a miser, and acts irrationally. Economists know better and perhaps this is why so many are penniless! Anyone who collects world currency or old coins instead of stamps is seeing those items not as money, for purchasing power, but as physical works of art.

Works of art are like all other commodities in that they offer scarcity value. One Van Gogh has more value because it is unique, and it loses value if imitated by a batch of identical counterfeits. It is the same with money. Counterfeiters erode the scarcity value of official currency and undermine public confidence in it. This has been used, once or twice, as one of the more successful features of wartime espionage. As Keynes said, 'there is no more successful way to undermine the nation than to debauch the currency'. But Keynes was not referring to undercover work by foreign agents against another country; he had in mind the actions of the country's own government itself!

The missing element in the discussion so far on money and inflation is government. Banks create money through deposits, partial reserves and loans, and the amount of money sets its value in simple terms of reduced relative scarcity. A fall in the value of money in exchange for goods and services is inflation, which may result in undesirable effects on international competitiveness and fixed income earners. But where is the role of government in all this? In fact the government is deeply involved at almost every step along the way.

The government is responsible for maintaining the national currency in adequate supply, and acceptable value. Its agency in this is the Bank of England, the Old Lady of Threadneedle Street, who issues new notes and coin and claims back the old, and watches over the banking system. But being watched by an Old Lady is not going to be enough to control the safety and performance of such a complicated financial centre these days. Effective, if often discreet action is needed as well. Action to influence the money supply can take different forms, some of which are highly technical. In approach, however, the policy is quite straightforward: to restrict the availability of cash and other reserves and to push up interest rates in order to squeeze bank lending, or vice versa. The government's own involvement in these areas on a day-to-day basis gives them the best opportunity to exert influence in these ways.

Suppose there is too much bank lending, a consumer credit boom and a crisis for the balance of payments and inflation. The government is the largest borrower in the land, through the National Debt, so can restructure its borrowing to raise demand, and so interest rates for short-term loans. It can adjust its own dealings with banks in order to restrain the growth of notes and coin and other reserves into banks until this again pushes up interest rates and cuts public borrowing. It introduces a credit squeeze. It can use its influence in other aspects of economic policy, such as taxation, the Budget and public borrowing, to tackle the underlying forces in the economy that caused the increase in bank credit in the first place. But will it choose to do so? Probably it will, but this depends on the view taken on one of the most contentious issues in contemporary economics – the nature of monetary inflation.

Monetarism and How to Live With It

One of the oldest and most durable ideas in economics is stated by the quantity theory of money: that changes in the real supply of money set proportional changes in the general level of prices, so excess monetary growth causes inflation. Monetarists see this relationship justified in theory, as people choose to spend their excess money balances thus pulling market prices up, and in practice from statistical observations of many different economies over many different periods of time. Milton Friedman is accredited with having promoted this view to its contemporary prominence, and he quotes evidence to support the theory from many sources including those in Figure 6.1. Certainly it appears that, over a period of years, the rise in real money supply is closely related to the rise in prices.

The relationship between money and prices is not really surprising. Relative value depends on relative scarcity in this as in all other spheres of economics. Money exchanges for goods and if more money exchanges for the same amount of goods then the value of each unit of money must have fallen. Too much money chases too few goods. Cheap money implies dear goods. The rise in the prices of all goods is the same thing as a fall in the value of money. What is contested by critics of monetarism, however, is whether the amount of goods might grow rather than remain the same, whether the extra money might be hoarded rather than spent and if so for how long, and whether the money and prices are both set by other forces in the economy. At its extreme monetarism predicts not only that money

FIGURE 6.1
Money and Prices

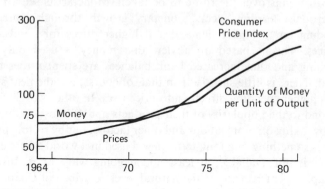

SOURCE   from 'A Monetarist View' by Milton Friedman in
Money Talks, ed. Alan Horrox and Gillian McCredie, published
by Thames Methuen, London, 1983, p. 8.

sets prices but also that it is only money that sets prices, and that
money can only end up setting prices. The truth, the whole truth and
nothing but the truth.

In practice, monetarism is more flexible and pragmatic. Extra
money is needed by the economy to pay for extra goods produced
through investment and economic growth in the normal way.
Inflation may be affected by people's expectations of future pay and
price rises, as may the passing effects of monetary growth on output
and jobs. Thus government policy should aim to control only what it
sees as excess monetary growth. It should aim for a constant real
money supply, and use its influence over the banks as well as its
direct issue of notes and coin in order to achieve this. But it should
also seek to increase public appreciation of the inflationary process
and to correct distorted expectations about future price levels. This
means publishing and promoting monetary growth targets and
monetarist analysis. Some might claim that it is this public relations
aspect of monetarism that matters most in policy terms: if people
believe in monetarism then it works.

On Routes and Obstacles

Much of the disagreement about the significance of monetary growth begins over the route to be taken. Monetarists see a fairly direct path leading excess monetary growth through increased spending on to higher demand and higher prices for goods and services. This is based on a view that money is used only for spending and that increased bank balances are spent rather than saved. There is little surprising in that, of course, but the next stage leads higher spending directly into price rises. In other words, firms respond to the popularity of their products not by boosting output, not by taking on more labour and other factors, but by raising price. This is something of a long-term view, based in a world where extra labour is not available, at least not at going wage rates. Instead unemployment remains at the natural level described in Chapter 2, and output grows at the natural rate for the economy as set by investment and technical improvements.

What other route could monetary growth follow? One probability is that higher consumer spending will go on imports, possibly to a large extent. British consumers enjoy spending on hi-fis, videos, cameras and holidays in the sun, all of which invite them to spend abroad. So imports may rise and the balance of payments get worse. A payments deficit could prompt a fall in the exchange rate of the pound, and that kicks up importers' prices and home firms' profits and wage settlements. This pattern of spending is likely to lead swiftly and surely to a rise in prices, but there is an alternative route that places many more obstacles in the way of monetary inflation. It is this last possibility that leads many economists to doubt the significance. or at least the certainty of monetarist predictions.

Suppose people decide their spending not on the basis simply of their current bank balance but instead on a more fundamental assessment of their income now, or in the past, or as expected in future? This would then determine their claims for notes and coin to withdraw from their bank accounts, and their decisions to spend or save. The level of money supply would be incidental, perhaps growing in response to spending demand but possibly not. People could still spend more by simply spending their cash more quickly and withdrawing more often from banks. Suppose, furthermore, that people choose to save rather than spend spare cash. This could be lent out to investors and spent by them, or it could be hoarded if people speculated that their money might gain value, through improved lending opportunities or falling prices, in this way. Even if investors spend the money, so raising demand for goods and services, this might employ spare and previously unemployed resources in the economy. National output and employment could rise instead of prices, at least for a time. This is a route, therefore, with many side-turnings and obstructions. Monetary growth may still be inflationary or it may not. It may affect growth and employment or it may, for a time perhaps, affect the economy in no significant way at all. It depends.

Policy and Targets

Excess monetary growth is likely, sooner or later, to cause inflation. Governments have tended to respond to this threat with angry determination. They make announcements to develop public awareness of the problem and support for whatever unpleasant policies are needed to overcome it. They assemble a package of policies to tackle the causes of inflation, however those are identified, and to soften the impact on other weakened patients in the economic infirmary: growth, jobs or the balance of payments. Then they pick up their weapons and attack. But the enemy is well disguised and protected. It is not an easy matter to decide exactly where and how inflation has been caused. There is a temptation for the government to vent its wrath on whatever guilty-looking suspect first comes its way.

The battle against inflation in the 1980s was fought on two main fronts: monetary growth and public sector borrowing. The Chancellor of the Exchequer announced targets for these two in his spring Budget each year. These targets were laid out for the following three years as the headlines for the Medium Term Financial Strategy (MTFS). The aim was progressively to reduce the levels of both in order to squeeze inflation from the economy. Table 6.2 shows the targets as they were announced from year to year.

The MTFS targets were used to describe the government's monetary and fiscal policies, therefore, in broad summary terms. Monetary policy involves the government, through the Bank of England, in altering interest rates, bank lending and monetary growth. There are many types of loans, levels of interest rates and forms of banking

TABLE 6.2
The Medium Term Financial Strategy

Targets announced in Budget statement each year, for following three financial years

	Monetary Growth % per annum		PSBR % of GDP		
1979	7–11	(£M3)	$4\frac{3}{4}$		
1980	7–11		$3\frac{3}{4}$		
1981	6–10		$4\frac{1}{4}$		
1982	8–12		$3\frac{1}{2}$		
1983	7–11		$2\frac{3}{4}$		
1984	6–10		$2\frac{1}{4}$		
1985	5–9	3–7 (M0)	2		
1986	11–15	2–6	$1\frac{1}{4}$		
1987		2–6	1		
1988		1–5	(1)		$-\frac{3}{4}$*
1989		1–5	(1)	(0)	$-2\frac{3}{4}$
1990		0–4	(1)	(0)	$-1\frac{3}{4}$
1991		0–4		(0)	-1
1992		–1–3			$-\frac{1}{2}$

*Original targets amended in subsequent Budgets.
SOURCE　*Budget Statements* (London: HMSO).

business, so any single measure can only give a general impression of the government's aims. Taking that measure to be one for monetary growth, however, introduces a more acute problem.

We have seen that the definition of money is a flexible, functional one: essentially, money is as money does. Notes and coin are counted as cash, but so too are bank 'sight' accounts that can be used to make cheque payments. Some other bank accounts are also seen as money, or something very close to it. The government first set as its MTFS target the rate of growth of '£M3', which includes most bank accounts whether offering cheque books or not. When this misbehaved and started to be used as a speculative investment rather than money, the government changed its target to a much narrower, purer definition of 'M0' which includes just notes and coin, not bank accounts.

Fiscal policy covers government action to steer the economy through its public expenditure and taxation and the balance, or more likely imbalance between them. This Budget balance has usually been in deficit as a Public Sector Borrowing Requirement (PSBR) but turned in the late 1980s into a surplus, a debt repayment. We will return to this area in more detail in the next chapter on the Budget and macroeconomic management. For the present, it should be appreciated how significant this borrowing/repayment might be for the monetary sector.

Public borrowing, for instance, is financed by selling financial securities and paying a rate of interest. If those securities are taken up as investments by the general public, they raise demand for loan funds and boost interest rates. If taken up by banks, those that are short term can be held as liquid reserves and be used to promote further bank credit and monetary growth. If retained by the Bank of England, they are used to back the issue of new notes and coin, which is printing more money. Thus public borrowing, depending on how it is financed, can cause an excessive growth of the money supply, and inflation. Controlling public borrowing or converting it into a National Debt repayment may help to defeat inflation.

Has Policy Succeeded?

Governments like to be able to claim success. In the battle against inflation, they have won two victories in particular. One is in concentrating public attention on the enemy of inflation, even while other dangers were close beside: slump, unemployment, and manufacturing decline. The message has come across that inflation deserves priority even in this company, and furthermore that inflation may be a cause of these other problems. The second success is also a tribute to what is now called presentation, but at other times has been called propaganda. The education campaign of monetarism has raised this aspect of economics also in the public consciousness. Many people who have little experience of economics now accept the connection between monetary growth and price rises. More importantly, industrialists and union leaders involved in pricing and pay decisions watch the money figures, and take them into account in negotiations. In many respects, monetarism has become accepted doctrine.

Yet this is surprising because the performance of monetary figures and inflation targets in the monetarist age has been far from consistent. The government has not always practised as it has preached. Inflation was brought down over a number of years, especially from 1980 to 1983 but at other times it has risen, sometimes quite sharply. Clearly, there have been problems along the way. It has proved difficult to identify money supply and to control it accurately enough, especially from month to month. This problem has become enshrined in a tribute to the economic commentator William Goodhart in terms of his 'law' that whatever is defined as the monetary target becomes immediately uncontrollable. Monetary markets are too flexible and sophisticated to lie subject to government control for very long.

Other economic influences have blown the government's targets off course. First, the slump cut tax receipts and increased dole payments, to raise the PSBR too high; then boom raised tax-takes and job creation to convert it into a debt repayment, almost by surprise. The government's own policies in other areas have sometimes intruded, as with structural reforms to financial markets in the early 1980s, and tax cuts, exchange rate intervention and other incentives to personal credit in the late 1980s. These changes can make it difficult to interpret the figures on money and borrowing as they come in, but also they make it more difficult to achieve the targets set for reasons of counter-inflationary control alone.

Behind it all there lies a problem with the nature of inflation itself. However it may begin, inflation continues in a self-perpetuating cycle. A rise in wage costs leads firms to push up their product prices, which raises the cost of living and leads workers to press for wage rises once more. The going rate of inflation is taken by all parties to be the starting point for their next pay or price increase. The spiral of inflation encourages them to expect it to continue, and to try always to get ahead of others with the next increase. Thus the expectation of inflation, to all but pure monetarists, is probably enough to cause inflation on its own.

The UK seems to have caught this habit of inflationary thinking. Inflation has been a persistent problem for the UK economy through good years and bad, right-wing and left-wing governments, one set of policies and another. This inflation has usually been higher than in competitor countries, as reflected in the compensating decline of the exchange rate from $4.80 to $1.50 in the post-war period. Monetarism has not been applied more successfully in the UK than in other countries and inflation finished the 1980s still high, still tending to rise. Perhaps the time has come to consider once more the alternative approaches that may be tried in the 1990s.

Controlling Demand

Inflation is a rise in the general price level but, as such, is comprised of many individual price rises. Each good, service and form of work experiences a rise in its price within a single circuit of inflation. Inflation can be seen to arrive like a rain cloud, in a single downpour made up of countless individual drops. Each drop can be seen on its own, and each price rise can be explained, as in Chapter 3, by market forces of supply and demand. This approach to inflation allows us to explain it as, essentially, resulting either from a demand or a supply change. This is illustrated in Figure 6.2. The main difference exposed by this market theory is whether the rise in price is accompanied by a rise in output, as economic growth and job creation, or a fall in output, as slump and unemployment. The stormcloud of inflation can herald a rainbow of economic boom or the low pressure of a depression.

Consider a rise in demand throughout the economy. This will appear as a rise in spending on all goods and services together. Firms try to take on more workers, machines and other factors to meet the demand. If it was only one of them this might succeed, but taken all together it results in competition for finite resources, and pulls up wages, interest and other costs. The tendency is for output and employment to rise if possible, then for prices to rise. But what might cause such a general rise in spending in the first place? Monetarists believe that inflation is 'always and everywhere a monetary phenomenon' so any demand rise is attributable to excessive monetary growth. Critics of monetarism say that the problem starts before that point in a change in people's spending

FIGURE 6.2
Demand and Cost Inflation

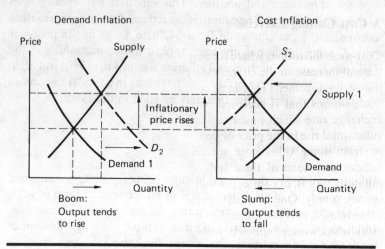

behaviour, to which the money supply simply responds. Perhaps the government increases its planned spending for political reasons, or investors plan to buy new machinery in the expectation of future good times. Assuming that the economy is at full capacity the result is demand-pull inflation.

To control it the government seeks to control demand in the economy and spending in general. Deflationary policy cuts spending in a number of ways: fiscal policy reduces government spending and raises taxation, leading to a Budget surplus, and monetary policy raises interest rates and cuts bank credit and other lending. Each control may hit different, specific targets at first, such as higher rate income tax payers or consumer credit, but as that group's spending affects firms, employees and their spending it quickly spills over to the rest of the economy as well. The choice of controls depends more on the government's other concerns, perhaps, or on the relative speed and effectiveness of each form of deflation. If the government has committed itself to low tax rates and an announced public spending programme, it may rely instead on a credit squeeze to work through interest rates and monetary growth. However it is finally packaged, deflationary policy to curb excess demand is likely to remain as the main weapon, albeit an unsatisfactory one, to fight inflation in the 1990s.

A Cost Cutting Exercise

Cost-push inflation is where the spiral of cost-price rises starts with a general increase in the charges for production facing all firms in all industries together. This may come through wage pressure from trade unions that is accepted by employers, or from a fall in the exchange rate which pushes up import costs. It may come from a substantial rise in the price of one important commodity such as oil, or from some other cost source altogether. Monetarists would believe that none of these influences could prompt a continuing inflation, unless, of course, it was financed by excessive growth of the money supply. One particular price rise would instead be offset by other relative cuts elsewhere. But if inflationary expectations become established, as can happen in wage bargaining or pricing up imports, it may take some time for long-term market forces to regain control. In the meantime, costs rise, prices rise, sales drop and slumpflation takes hold.

The interventionist, non-monetarist governments of the 1960s and 1970s were well aware of this danger and responded with a range of policies. These included demand deflation, but at a further cost to spending, output and jobs. The cost of curing inflation this way, when already in a national slump, can seem unacceptably high. The alternative they turned to was called prices and incomes policy but, in effect, amounted to two main measures. One was to limit wage rises, especially in the public sector, more than price rises. This amounted to deflation again, but on a selective basis and under another name. The other was to attack inflationary expectations with a high profile agreement, and proposed enforcement, to limit national wage and price settlements. Typically, this involved unions and employers' groups in cooperation with the government. An initial 'freeze' hit expectations hardest, to be followed by progressively more relaxed 'norms' for rises.

Prices and incomes policy helped to control inflation, at least for a time, and at less of a cost in terms of deflation. It attracted something of a bad name, however, even before the fashion turned to monetarist discipline. This was partly due to its disguised, partial deflation and the fact that it was successful only with some forms of incomes – typically the lower rates, in the public sector. The problem was mainly one of bottling up economic pressures, so that inflation took off faster than ever as the policy collapsed. Controls were too inflexible to accommodate long-term allocative arrangements, to pay highly productive workers more or to raise relative price for goods in current demand. Perhaps the 1990s will see a return to these sorts of consensus, moral suasion policies, especially if inflation weathers the monetarist era unscathed. Certainly, the need to control expectations remains a top priority, if only to allow monetarist discipline to take effect without cost to the level of economic activity.

What Is the Cost of Controlling Inflation?

In a perfect world money would be under the control of the official authorities and inflation would be controlled at no cost to other government targets. The rate of growth of the money supply would be set by banks under the guidance of the Bank of England to match the real growth of demand for it in terms of increased output of goods and services. Inflation would not occur, but if as a mistake it did this could be rectified through the rate of growth of money. People's expectations of inflation would adjust immediately and correspondingly, and with no effect on production, job offers or real employment. How relieved the government would be, if indeed there needed to be any government at all! But this is science fiction, or nostalgia. The current state of the economy is altogether more complicated. The fact of life today is that it costs the government dearly to control inflation.

National spending affects more than just demand inflation. Deflationary policy is a double-edged sword and cuts more than just inflation. Every blow at the target of low inflation draws blood from the economy in lower economic growth and job losses. At least that was the convention accepted by governments, however unwillingly, until the 1980s. Analysis of spending in the national economy followed the lines laid down by Keynes in the 1930s, as we will see in the next chapter on macroeconomics. Policy trade-offs were summed up in terms of the Phillips curve relationship between wage inflation and labour unemployment, first identified in 1959. Deflationary policy such as tax and interest rate rises would cut spending and cut inflation, but at the cost of higher unemployment and recession. Reflationary policy to stimulate demand would do the opposite. These options are shown in Figure 6.3. The government might be able to minimise its losses but losses there would be, as one policy target was traded off against another.

Another problem would spring from international issues to do with the balance of payments and exchange rate. Deflation or reflation has a role to play here as well for domestic spending attracts imports and interest rates on bank accounts attract foreign deposits. Deflation to cure rising prices, therefore, would have the side-effect of a stronger balance of payments and higher exchange rate. In the longer term this might damage the country's competitive position and trading performance. Britain has had ample experience of just this effect. Recurring payments and inflation crises from the 1950s to the 1970s, virtually until the sanctuary offered by North Sea oil, forced successive governments' hands. The cost in deindustrialisation and weakened foreign trade performance is still being felt. The relationship between internal and external balance is possibly

FIGURE 6.3
The Phillips Curve

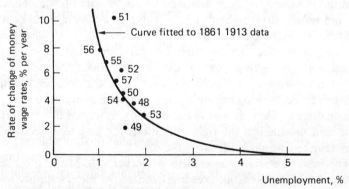

1948-57, with unemployment lagged 7 months

SOURCE   A. W. Phillips, 'Unemployment and Wage Rates', *Economica*, vol. 25 (1958) pp. 283–99.

even closer now. A high interest rate policy to cure inflation attracts vast inflows from abroad into the City, raising the exchange rate. Indeed this is intentional since a strong pound keeps import prices down. But at how great a cost in trading performance, growth and jobs?

The Wrath of God

The economic climate changed in the 1980s. A cold wind described variously as realism and dogmatism blew through the corridors of power. It swept away traditional economic values of compromise and compassion. In terms of economic policy, it asserted that inflation should be controlled at whatever cost and, anyway, accepted opinions about what that cost would be were wrong. If there seemed to be a lack of economic objectivity in this, a return to values be they Victorian or Thatcherite, then that was no accident. The control of inflation was indeed seen as a moral question.

This centred on the issue of inflation's relationship with the rest of the economy, or rather the lack of it. Monetarists see inflation as a purely monetary issue. Limiting the growth of the money supply should affect only the general level of prices. Trade-off effects on growth and employment could arise only by mistake, as people misinterpreted their levels of pay or spending and failed to adjust to realistic expectations. The Phillips curve would work only temporarily and only a short-sighted, irresponsible government would subscribe to it. Indeed, the danger with inflation was quite otherwise: the long-term effect was to harm competitiveness and discourage investment, so cutting growth and causing unemployment. The outward movements of the Phillips curve over the decades, linking rising inflation to rising unemployment, was seen as evidence for this British disease. The cure was to end inflation, at whatever temporary cost, and to establish the right conditions for long-term recovery. Anything less would be ducking the issue.

The moral question was seen to go deeper still. Monetarists see that inflation results from excess growth of the money supply and that the money supply is the responsibility of government. In fact the government promotes that growth through printing money, backed by government borrowing, to pay for its public expenditure. But the effect of inflation is to cut the value of fixed interest earnings, such as those received from loans to the government as bonds. Moreover, the government is the largest borrower in the land, largely in this form. What we have here, therefore, might be described as economic theft. The government stands accused on two counts. First, it prints money to raise finance for its expenditure that does not have to be authorised by Parliament. Secondly, it causes inflation from which it is the main beneficiary. In this sense it steals purchasing power, without constitutional authority, from its own citizens.

From this point of view inflation is an evil, and the wrath of God should descend upon it. In such a spirit the battle against inflation begins. But perhaps there are other problems that also need addressing, and that claim priority over inflation, especially as it falls to acceptable levels? Until it rises once more and again becomes public enemy number one!

Control of the Economy – Just Good Housekeeping? 7

One way in which Mrs Thatcher's governments in the 1980s have been remarkable is in their attitude to the Budget. They have led public opinion towards attitudes of prudent financing and good housekeeping in the expressed belief that this would encourage growth and prosperity. The return to Victorian values has embraced those that Mr Micawber aspired to but so sadly neglected: 'annual income twenty pounds, annual expenditure nineteen nineteen six, result happiness. Annual income twenty pounds, annual expenditure twenty pounds ought and six, result misery.'

The Budget is the statement of government tax revenue, borrowing and other receipts such as those from privatisation asset sales. This is presented to Parliament in March at the start of each financial year to show how the government intends to pay for forthcoming expenditure. The statement attracts a great deal of attention and analysis largely because it is seen as the main guide to official policy on controlling the economy. Along with the immediate changes in personal tax rates and excise duties that attract the limelight from the media, there is much detailed and technical information. But the bottom line in economic terms is the overall balance between government spending and revenue – in other words, the projected level of public borrowing for the forthcoming year. If expenditure exceeds revenue, as was the case for most of the 1960s, 1970s and 1980s, the government must borrow money to buy its Budget deficit, and run a Public Sector Borrowing Requirement (PSBR). If tax revenue is greater than expenditure the government runs a Budget surplus and can afford to pay back some of its loans from other years – the National Debt – with a Public Sector Debt Repayment (PSDR).

PSBR/DR is the financial statement of net borrowing or lending over a given fiscal year (see Table 7.1). This will add to or subtract from the accumulated value of all past government borrowing: the National Debt. Most borrowing is by the central government departments such as the Department of Education and Science and the Ministry of Defence, but the public sector also includes local authorities such as the London Boroughs and the County of Kent, as well as public corporations such as British Rail and the BBC. Public borrowing may be financed in alternative ways by selling government securities, either short-term Treasury bills or long-term stocks, to banks, or the general public. We saw in the last chapter how sales of securities to the Bank of England leads to an increased and possibly inflationary printing of money. But the PSBR/DR may give a misleading indication of the government's true financial position due to the inclusion of once and for all asset sales, as part of privatisation.

The Budget of 1988 stands out in modern times as the first year in

TABLE 7.1
PSBR in the UK

Financial Year	PSBR as % GDP
1979–80	5
1980	$5\frac{1}{2}$
1981	$3\frac{1}{2}$
1982	$3\frac{1}{4}$
1983	$3\frac{1}{4}$
1984	3
1985	$1\frac{1}{2}$
1986	1
1987	$-\frac{3}{4}$
1988	-3

SOURCE *Budget Statements* (London: HMSO).

which the Chancellor of the Exchequer could announce a surplus – a PSDR. After many years of seeking to reduce public spending and to eliminate public borrowing he must have felt proud to claim, ahead of his MTFS target, that 'the strength of the economy coupled with fiscal prudence has enabled the government to achieve a balanced budget on a sustainable basis'. But of course the Budget did not balance so much as transfer from deficit to surplus, and only time would show the durability of this new position.

So how may it be better for the government to run a surplus or a deficit? Those favouring fiscal prudence usually see the government's position as being very like that of an individual citizen in the economy. You need to balance your spending with your income, at least in the long term. You will probably justify overspending on a particular large item, such as a house bought on a mortgage or a car on hire purchase, and borrow for a limited time to cover the difference. At other times, you may save up to buy the stereo or clothes that you have chosen. It may be all too easy to run up excessive debts, but prudent financing requires that you spend only up to your budget.

Similar fiscal prudence on the part of the government would match tax revenue to total public expenditure, preferably excluding once off revenue from asset sales. But should long-term investment in public sector projects be financed from current revenue in the way implied for MTFS targets? Probably it would be more prudent still to allow for borrowing to finance any project that can produce an anticipated rate of return to society in excess of the rate of interest on the loan.

Dear Prudence

Neo-classical economists encourage the government to set a good example for its individual citizens by being financially self-sufficient. But Keynesian economists believe that the macroeconomic aggregates are connected in such a way that government intervention is needed to ensure good economic performance. A Budget deficit, for example, increases overall spending in the economy, stimulates growth and creates jobs in a time of slump. A Budget surplus, or even just balancing the Budget, can cut spending and curb inflation, or if taken too far, cut output and jobs.

These effects are difficult to predict because of the relationships between national aggregates. But one thing is clear: the government has the ability and the responsibility to compensate for other macroeconomic forces by using the Budget balance. Keynes showed in the 1930s what governments have generally understood since, that the Budget can be used as a tool of policy to act upon major targets such as growth and employment rather than as an end in itself. In this view a sustained bout of prudent financing can be disastrous. Balancing the Budget in a time of slump implies spending cuts which not only deepen the slump but may also lead ironically to falling tax-takes and a worse Budget position: a vicious circle of decline. Budget prudence may be achieved only at the cost of wrecking the economy.

The Targets of Government Policy

What is it that wins elections? In 1979, the dominant issue was inflation and the different policy approaches that could be used to control it. In 1987, the concern was much more for jobs and unemployment. But more important still, at almost every election, is the country's record on growth for if living standards are rising well, and perceived by the electorate to be likely to continue to rise, the current government stands a very good chance of retaining power. Perhaps this is why it is said that elections are won or lost by the government party, rather than the opposition. Of course, there are many important national issues besides these continuing economic ones, but we can generalise and say that the macroeconomic targets of government embrace these key aggregates: economic growth and the rise in living standards, unemployment and job creation, inflation of the general price level, and to a lesser extent the balance of payments and exchange rate of the pound. Why should they seem so significant?

It is partly the economist in all of us that makes us compare our lot: perhaps against the Jones next door, perhaps against what we had or did ourselves in the past. We like to feel that we are making progress, but when it comes to the general standard of living this can be difficult to assess. Cars, telephones, holidays, shows or gardens cannot be measured immediately against one another. At a national level there are enormous complications in trying to compare living standards in different places or at different times. The best that economists can do is to use official statistics of annual national income (such as Gross Domestic Product, GDP,) and adapt these to allow for changes or differences in the general level of prices, and population. Thus real national income per head is taken as the measure of material living standards, and a rise in that level from one time to another is the measure of real economic growth.

Jobs and Prices

Short-term advantages and disadvantages in national income can be bought or lost, however, in a way that disguises the true level of living standards. Growth can follow cyclical patterns with good years followed by bad and with actual performance that is disappointing by comparison with potential. Similarly, the balance of payments can signify that the country is currently living beyond or within its means. Unemployment implies that more could be produced if spare resources were all put to work; but there are other reasons as well for reading significance into unemployment statistics. Economic forces are built into the values and attitudes of our society in very many ways, but perhaps none so strongly as the work ethic. People are often identified and assessed by others in terms of the job they do – or their lack of any job at all. The issue of work and unemployment, and its historic significance since one extreme in the 1930s and the other extreme in the 1950s, is built deeply into political divisions between those on the left and those on the right. And the differences in lifestyle, in opportunities and aspirations of those in work and those out of work lead to divisions within families and between regions.

Clearly, jobs and unemployment are significant for the quality of national life in their own right, as well as for their impact on growth. But inflation is also important if it causes any of the adverse effects we observed in the last chapter – slump, payments deficit, or hardship for those on fixed incomes. Thus the targets of economic policy may stand on their own in some respects but they are also connected with each other.

Only the Economists Can Win

The economic forces that improve performance in one area almost certainly create problems in another. This certainly serves to keep life interesting for economists and for those involved in economic policy-making, for it is never possible to win on all counts at the same time. It can lead to a certain amount of cynicism, however, when economists give the impression that they only ever complain. Another complaint might be about the nature of economic advice: for every one economist there are at least two different opinions. In this case, the difference of opinion is one of the most controversial and crucial in contemporary economics. Which targets coincide and which are alternatives?

Keynesian economists see the performance of the macroeconomy in terms of spending, and it is spending that is the dominant force in controlling the behaviour of growth, unemployment, inflation and the balance of payments. As a general rule, therefore, higher spending brings more growth and jobs, but also inflation and imports. These four targets must be traded off against each other in the way implied in Figure 7.1. Neo-classical and monetarist econo-

FIGURE 7.1
The Targets of Policy

mists would not agree with this. They claim a longer term view where different areas of the economy are largely self-contained, and the control of inflation can be achieved without cost to growth or employment. Different policies may help each target but there is no common approach to affect all, unless it be in the absence of government intervention altogether.

Measuring UK Performance

Economists can start with a clear and simple question such as: 'how well has the UK performed in terms of growth, unemployment, inflation and the balance of payments?' In no time at all, however, the talk will have turned to technical language that can sound like nonsense to the uninitiated: 'it all depends on NNP at factor cost, surely . . .'; 'the TPI is an altogether more reliable indicator than the RPI, even when seasonally adjusted'; 'but the balance of visible trade is only a subcomponent of the current account'. This sort of technical language has its place in the subject in the same way that thermometer and air-pressure readings are used in weather forecasting. But it should still be possible to make sense of a weather report before you go out for the day. So how might we sum up the state of the economic climate?

Economic growth is counted by figures of the change of GDP from one year to the next. Gross Domestic Product (GDP) measures the value of all the goods and services produced by a country over a period of time. Typically, we are interested in annual production in real terms that allow for inflation rather than in money values alone, as shown in Table 7.2. Unemployment is usually measured as a percentage, showing the proportion of the available national workforce officially registered as being out of work, but the converse statistic of numbers in employment or of additional jobs being created is also valuable. Inflation is measured from the change in the official index of the average of consumer prices, where that weighted average is usually calculated quickly and often from a sample of the main products bought at a number of retail outlets.

The balance of payments is less self-explanatory than the other measures: for if all payments in and out of the country are counted these add up to zero. The foreign exchange market sets a perfect equilibrium exchange rate in the way we saw in Chapter 4 and so matches supply of pounds, resulting from outward payments, to demand for pounds, resulting from inward payments. But individual sections of the account can be in surplus or deficit, and it is the current account section that best reflects the country's trading position in goods and services alone. This can be counted in terms of pounds or, for comparison from time to time or country to country, as a percentage of national income (GDP).

Taking the Good With the Bad

'Looking ahead, I expect 1988 to be yet another year of healthy growth with low inflation; and there is every prospect that unemployment will continue to fall.' How proud the Chancellor must have been that he could use these words in his Budget speech in 1988, and how pleased any government would be to succeed in terms of all the different macroeconomic targets at the same time. Prime Minister Edward Heath was to claim in 1973 that 'our only problem at the moment is the problem of success', just four months before the Winter of Discontent, the three-day week and his election defeat. But such pleasure is typically short-lived to judge by the record shown in Table 7.2.

Compared to the UK's previous performance, the 1980s have indeed seen a period of excellent, sustained economic growth. But at

TABLE 7.2
Performance of the UK Economy (selected years)

	Growth (% change in real GDP)	Unemployment (% of labour force. Figures amended 1983 on)	Inflation (% rise in retail prices)	Balance of Payment (Current Balance, £000m)
1980	− 2.3	6.8	18.0	+ 3.1
1984	+ 1.8	10.7	5.0	+ 2.1
1988	+ 3.7	8.2	4.9	− 14.9

SOURCE *Economic Trends* (London: HMSO, 1989).

the same time the level of unemployment reached unprecedented heights. Even on inflation, where the government might have claimed its greatest success in cutting the rate from 18 to 3 per cent, this performance has failed to match that in major competing countries. Their inflation started lower, but also remained lower as inflation rates were brought down around the world. And the strong growth of domestic demand has sucked in imports like never before, so turning a record balance of payments surplus at the start of the 1980s into a clear deficit.

Were things better in the past? Nostalgia leads us naturally to suppose that they were, and that our problems are new problems, and more difficult because they are ours. The 1950s are remembered by the catchphrase attributed to the then Prime Minister Harold Macmillan: 'you've never had it so good'. That also was a time of good growth, low unemployment and low inflation. But repeated balance of payments crises lead to cycles of stop-go economic management. Strong growth would lead to excessive imports and current account deficit until the government felt obliged to raise interest rates and taxes to choke off demand for all including imports.

Perhaps the main question should be about the role of government. What does explain the performance of the economy and how far can this be attributed to the policies of one government or another? Economists disagree about the answers to these questions as they do about most others, but in particular they disagree about the direction of policy: whether the government improves performance more by increasing intervention or by stepping aside and leaving the economy to function more on its own.

The Supply-side Approach

The view that the economy works best if left to itself has a long pedigree. Adam Smith, the father of the subject that we recognise as economics, began the blood line when he talked of the invisible hand of capitalism. Students of Western economics still start their study of the subject by looking at individual markets and the free market forces of supply and demand. These forces work in a way described by another great economist, Alfred Marshall, as the twin blades of a pair of scissors to set the price of each type of good, service or factor of production in each market. And it is these price signals that signify relative values and so determine the way resources are used and incomes distributed throughout the economy.

The classical view of economics, as it has become known, is essentially concerned with microeconomics but its implications for the macroeconomy are a natural and consistent extension: that aggregate variables such as national output, investment and unemployment are each determined by market forces within their own national markets. The most important of which would be those for national output, employment, capital investment, money and the balance of payments and exchange rate. Thus wage rates will adjust to match the supply of workers to firms' demand for labour, and the rate of interest will match the supply of funds to firms' demand for investment. The economy will automatically set its natural levels of employment and growth accordingly.

Lesser *Laissez-faire*

What goes wrong? Unemployment, slumps, exchange rate crises and so forth just should not occur in an efficient, free market world. Those who believe in classical economic ideas put the blame on imperfections that distort the signals sent to and from markets, or prevent markets from achieving their desired result. Trade unions are blamed, for example, for keeping their members' wages too high and so discouraging firms from creating enough jobs to employ everyone else. Above all, however, they blame government. Government policies often introduce the worst distortions, by paying benefits for those on low or non-existent earnings, by running a PSBR that keeps interest rates too high, by subsidising inefficient firms in the private and public sectors, and in many other ways.

Laissez-faire economists, therefore, generally prefer the government to follow a policy of non-policy. Ideally the government would introduce no market distortions of its own and would leave free market forces to be sovereign in the economy. But those associated with the recent resurgence of these ideas – the new-classical economists – accept that this ideal is no longer practical. There are too many other distortions in markets that the government has a responsibility to correct, by helping workers to retrain for newly created jobs or reversing the process of decline in inner city areas, for example. There are also particular responsibilities that the government can never shed, for defence, law and order, the environment, welfare and to an extent education and health as well.

In all these areas there is a common theme: the concern to ensure an adequate and efficient supply of resources to each market. Supply-side policies, as they have become known, include a host of apparently very different measures such as tax and benefits reform, more flexible housing and training, deregulation of state monopolies, and much more. The differences lie in the separate markets affected by each, but the common approach is to supply resources at least cost and to best effect. Not least in all this is the obligation on government to supply its own services to the community in the most efficient way possible, which brings us back once more to the notion of good housekeeping as a rule for good government.

The Keynesian Alternative

Modern macroeconomics was born, in a sense, amid the turmoil of the years spanning the two world wars. Before then orthodox economics had followed classical lines and stressed the self-balancing forces of free market economics. The slump and unemployment that came and remained to afflict the developed world for much of that period showed that these forces were no longer working satisfactorily. The depression served as a catalyst for the development of an alternative model of the economy, one now associated inextricably with the economist John Maynard Keynes.

This view stresses the interdependence of the areas of the macroeconomy and shows how changes in money markets can affect interest rates, which can affect investment, which can affect growth and jobs and unemployment or inflation. Market forces may ordain a cut in wages for certain workers, but Keynesian economics goes a step further to show how one group's pay cut affects their spending and so everyone else's production and jobs. The effects can be more severe than at first appears because these knock-on effects are repeated again and again. An initial cut in spending called, nationally, Aggregate Demand, has what is called a multiplied effect on production and employment in the economy. This is illustrated in Figure 7.2, where the vertical cut in spending plans brings an eventual, larger, horizontal cut in equilibrium national output.

FIGURE 7.2
The Multiplier

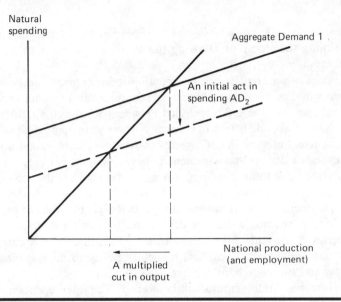

Keynesian economics is characterised by an intrinsic orientation towards government policy issues. Free market economics is all well and good in the right conditions, but if the conditions are not right, as was clearly the case in the 1930s, what should be done then? The new classical economists respond by trying to remove what they identify as imperfections in order to work for long-run improvements. Keynesian economics looks for more immediate solutions. This difference comes into sharp focus on two issues in particular. The first is about the time-scale for adjustment, which may stretch to a good number of years on problems such as international uncompetitiveness or mass unemployment. Free market economics may allow for a long-term solution; Keynes' response was that 'in the long-term we are all dead', and that short-term intervention was desirable if this could succeed. The second important issue is over the behaviour of prices and wages. It was clear in the 1930s that wages would not be allowed to drop as market economics required in order to create jobs. Keynesian economics accepted that as a working assumption and went on to show how the government might initiate recovery and multiplied job creation as an alternative approach.

Priming the Pump or Blowing the Well?

Keynesian economists are interventionist by nature. The governments that best lead their countries' economies away from international slump in the 1930s included President Roosevelt's USA with its New Deal and Hitler's in Germany. There were many differences, of course, but they shared aspects of what would be called now a Keynesian demand-management policy. This concentrates on the central role of total spending, or aggregate demand in the economy, for aggregate demand sets national output which sets the level of employment. The government can use its Budget to influence overall spending, running a Budget deficit and borrowing to finance increases in spending either on its own part or, through tax cuts, by private individuals. It can use monetary policy to depress interest rates and stimulate bank lending.

How much intervention will be needed? The interdependence of variables in Keynesian world suggests that government may need to offer little more than a lead, a kick start to get the motor working. In an age more accustomed to wells than to Model T Fords this approach was described for the New Deal as 'priming the pump'. Initial government reflation improves business expectations and has multiplied effects on spending. This generates extra tax revenue later. But all this contradicts the lessons of monetarism: can governments really expand the PSBR and money supply without turning the growth and employment they desire into inflation instead?

What is clear is that the slumps of the 1970s and 1980s have differed significantly from those that Keynes was analysing. Price levels have not been rigid, they have been rising fast as inflation coincided with slump. Reflation has not had a general, healing effect on the economy but has spilled quickly into dynamic and responsive sectors as it hits bottle-necks elsewhere. Thus the results have been seen more as inflation than falling unemployment, at least for a while, and also as a rise in imports and pressure on the pound. The external economy, as reflected in the balance of payments and exchange rate, has become increasingly involved with domestic issues of growth, inflation and unemployment. The British economy is 'open' to the world.

Open Economy Macroeconomics

Classical economics identifies separate markets, including those for the pound and other currencies used in foreign exchange. Changes in trading flows of exports and imports lead to changes in demand and supply for each currency and therefore a change in the equilibrium exchange rate of the pound. This is the rate at which one pound sterling can be exchanged for dollars or francs, or other currencies through banks or other money changers. With a free and perfect market left to its own devices these changes will automatically bring demand and supply, trade and other credits and debits, into balance. Thus the balance of payments and exchange rate of the pound find their own correct value with no need for government assistance and no necessary impact on the domestic economy. The government can concentrate on sound financial discipline and supply-side reform at home, leaving the external economy to take care of itself.

Keynesian economics is concerned with the interrelationships between economic forces and targets. Changes to international payments and exchange, therefore, are both determined by domestic events and an influence on them. An expansion of domestic demand, for example, attracts imports and leads to a payments deficit. This in turn tends to depress the exchange rate, which jacks up import prices and cuts demand. But the scale and timing of these connections can complicate matters: equilibrium is not achieved smoothly, and perhaps not at all.

So what are the guidelines for government policy? The exchange rate has changed greatly in recent years, falling by a quarter from 1981 to 1987, rising at other times. But at no stage during all this was any exchange rate quoted as a given target of policy. Was it really left to fend for itself as this might imply, despite its significance for domestic firms' competitiveness and for imported price inflation? Of course not. The exchange rate was guided deliberately and on occasions substantially by discreet, official policy to influence inward and outward payments, through interest rates and use of the reserves.

Interest rates are seen primarily as an instrument of monetary policy to restrict monetary growth in the way described in Chapter 6. They also play a role in the more general, Keynesian scheme of things by affecting plans for investment spending and so demand for goods and services in the economy as a whole. But now they have a third impact on an open economy such as the UK, for interest rates can attract international funds into this country and its currency and away from others. Thus relatively high rates of interest keep up the exchange rate, and keep down competitiveness, growth, employment and prices.

The official reserves are held by the Bank of England for the government in the form of foreign currencies such as dollars, marks or gold. In a perfectly free, private foreign exchange market there would be no reason to do this, and the cost of holding money would make it undesirable. But as a source of intervention in the market these reserves are essential. They allow the authorities to sell foreign currency in exchange for buying pounds and so raise the market value of sterling, or to sell pounds and acquire dollars, etc. to keep down the exchange rate. Intervention policy may only work for a while, and to the extent allowed by the reserves, but its effect on competitiveness and inflation in the meanwhile can be really significant. It adds another weapon to the government's arsenal in the fight against irreconcilable targets of growth and employment, stable prices and a balance of trade.

Which Way to Turn?

The government faces a range of policy options, some that are based on classical, supply-side ideas and some that are Keynesian, that are always the same but also always changing. What are the main options to choose from?

It is easy and therefore tempting to think in terms of two-way divisions: up or down, left or right, night or day. The same binary approach to macroeconomic policy-making gives us the conventional division: monetarist or Keynesian. The terms may have changed but the alternatives remain much the same as they were in the inter-war years. Then it was a choice between balancing the budget and relying on the gold standard to ensure monetary stability along orthodox, classical lines or to arrange government intervention through a Budget deficit, state control of investment and job-creation projects, and other Keynesian techniques. The UK kept faith with the orthodoxy of the day and the inter-war depression worsened. Unemployment rose over 3 million.

Now the contestants are in the ring again, sixty years older, wiser, bloodied but unbowed. On the right in the blue corner stands the new-classical policy. This includes a package of supply-side reforms to improve the efficiency of markets generally and the work of trade unions, labour, share and property ownership in particular. Its macroeconomic policy is still dominated by monetarism and the need to control, or at least maintain public confidence that it can control the growth of the money supply, along with the prudent public financing implied by a balanced Budget. This is the champion of the 1980s and holds a fine record of previous successes, including the longest sustained period of post-war growth, record job creation (and earlier job losses) and almost the defeat of inflation.

The other contestant stands on the left in the red corner, representing demand management and government intervention along Keynesian lines. All this has been out of fashion for ten or twenty years in the UK but has been in practice overseas and is coming back revitalised. The package of policies starts with budgetary, taxation and public spending reforms to stimulate depressed sectors of the economy through fiscal reflation. Further intervention would bring industrial investment, fund management, and social welfare under increased government control, with possible supporting measures to limit rises in wages and prices and imports. This approach dominated the policies of different governments in the 1960s and 1970s. Why should policies be thought to be suitable for one period but not for another?

Fashions and Failures

Fashion plays a part in the sense that policy priorities change with the conditions of the time. Recession and unemployment was the main concern in the 1930s and so economists searched for theories to explain and policies to solve that. Inflation was the main worry in the late 1970s and early 1980s so monetarism gained prominence against this public enemy number one. As unemployment soared from 1 to 3 million that claimed more of the limelight, and so on.

Policy failures are also likely to cause changes in direction. Keynes was once criticised for changing his point of view but his reply was a lesson for all involved in economic policy-making: 'If I'm wrong I change; what do you do?' The trouble is that economic conditions change, sometimes quite quickly, to make the economic theories and policies for one period unsuitable for the next. It can be worse than that, however, when the policies used to solve one problem themselves change the performance of the economy and so create new problems instead. As people become accustomed to government demand-management to cure unemployment, for example, they become less sensitive to the pressure of market forces in the labour market. Inflationary expectations become built into their decisions instead.

In the end, we must expect policy to be determined not just by theoretical prediction, or by economic experience, but by values and opinions as well. Political issues become associated with the economic ones, in the way that free market, *laissez-faire* principles are espoused by the political right wing and interventionist, demand-management principles by the left. Independent policy-making agencies such as the Federal Reserve in the USA, or perhaps the European Commission in the EEC, can play down the political aspect of economic policy to an extent. For most of us the subject's appeal lies in the association of economic ideas and experience with important and controversial questions of political policy. But to the politicians involved it can be a tricky matter of timing to claim pride for today's economic successes before they turn into tomorrow's failures.

Economics – More Questions Than Answers?

8

Consider a success story of our times. In a sense the character is as old as the hills but is also found in any of the current TV soap operas. We love them, we hate them but also we aspire to be like them. They are the winners in today's society. They are easily recognised. They are ambitious and self-centred with a strong opinion of their own worth, in fact strong opinions on most things. They go their own way and woe betide anyone who stands against them, for they make dangerous enemies. But they win through, and win the support of others around them through their unquenchable determination to succeed, to gain power and influence.

What feeds this determination? They desire to have more than other people and to do better than other people, indulging themselves to excess. They can drink others under the table, outplay them at cards, win at any competition they choose to enter. What about time off? They like nothing better than to lie by the pool in Spain, or sip cold drinks on their yacht or steer their motorised lawnmower around the estate. Work is competitive success and leisure is inactivity. They may not be attractive or pleasant but they are winners, and their success brings admiration and support.

Who are these people, are they merely comic book characters from the soap operas? The TV series are too popular and strike too many chords with their audiences for that to be true. We recognise these qualities in our colleagues, rivals and bosses, if not in ourselves. Few people will offer many of these qualities but then few people achieve runaway success as in fictional TV. The most successful ones climb to the top of their career ladder and perpetuate their qualities in others. And they play a part, a large part in economics today. Economics is often described as a theoretical world of beings motivated only by self-interest. They act to maximise their own personal satisfaction with complete disregard of others. Economic beings respond to different situations with cold logic: working for maximum earnings, competing ruthlessly for market share and profit, buying and selling in markets for greatest personal advantage. Economic success brings income, wealth, power and profit.

But surely this is a complete fiction, or an exaggeration at least. Let us hope it is for the character described, as old as the hills and as familiar as all fiction, represents the seven deadly sins. He is pride, first and foremost. His arrogance and self-importance feeds anger at others, insatiable greed for wealth, and excessive self-indulgence or gluttony. Overweening self-regard brings envy of others' advantages, lustful appetite for what they have, and laziness or sloth. If we met these qualities in the street we would surely turn away. But would we call them sins? Economics relies on self-interest to motivate individuals to rational action, portrays leisure as non-work and work as non-fulfilment. This is the framework for objective and accurate decision-making that is used to answer the questions of economics today.

Decision-making Skills

Positive economics, as it is called, is the objective study of the behaviour of rational economic beings. It predicts the behaviour of individuals at work, as consumers and as producers, and builds a picture at the collective, general level of the performance of the macroeconomy. This excludes personal, subjective opinion and judgements of value. Questions of whether one distribution of income is better than another or one target preferable to another are brought in, to an extent, in normative economics. Introductory courses study only positive issues, however, and seek to train students to distinguish their own values and opinions from objective, indisputable logic. This is an invaluable training in a two-stage approach to decision-making.

Ask young children why they do something and they are likely to reply 'because we want to'. This level of decision-making is a matter of will rather than judgement, based on feeling rather than argument. Some management decisions, some decisions of economic policy can appear to be equally arbitrary, but most follow the decision-making process adopted in economic analysis. This starts with a clear purpose, a motive to initiate and direct action. Entrepreneurial firms seek to maximise their profits, governments to promote the welfare of their citizens, and consumers to gain the greatest personal satisfaction possible. Decisions are then considered as a choice between alternatives, and at the margin, between an option and its next best alternative. The marginal stage is most important in this, at all stages of economics. It allows us to predict an individual's movement in one direction or another, to add one more unit or take one off. This can then be continued, step by step, as long as we wish.

Then comes the theory. We construct a hypothetical model of behaviour. Given conditions, given motivation, imply a predictable pattern of decisions. These decisions may only be in the mind, as with a demand curve of intentions to buy at different price levels. They may be changed altogether by changes in conditions, as with a rise in consumer income causing a shift up of all intended demand. But the value of the model is in allowing comparisons and predicting behaviour under any and all circumstances. It offers flexibility of treatment but certainty of answer. But if the value of theory is as logical argument, the drawback is a lack of realism and lack of evidence. The last stage in decision-making is to observe factual evidence and interpret this data as proof for or against the predictions of different models. This is called applied economics. Taken further, where statistical data is used first to identify and quantify economic relationships, it is called econometrics.

Economic method requires skills of accurate observation, clear logical thought, coherent expression of ideas and arguments, and perceptive interpretation of evidence. These are first-class decision-making skills, valuable to any non-specialist economist who goes on to work in management, finance, law or administration. Suppose, for example, that you wish to throw a party. Set out with a purpose: is it to raise funds, or for people to meet each other, or so you can have fun? Weigh the alternatives: are you going to lay it all on yourself, ask others to help, have it at home or hire some place? Predict what will happen: if the right people come in a good frame of mind it will be a huge success, but if not it could become a riot.

Check these predictions against evidence and experience: what happened last time, or at someone else's party, or when the police were called!

A final decision invariably relies on judgement, or opinion to an extent. There is a stage, therefore, at which personality and values come in and, indeed, take over. The government is advised by economists what will happen to the economy under different sets of policies. It is a political judgement, however, as to which outcome for growth, jobs, prices and incomes is the more desirable. Similarly, economics shows how resources may be used most efficiently to achieve as much production as possible in an economy. It is a matter for personal judgement to prefer a distribution of incomes that is in favour of one group or another, or more or less even. The objective argument of economics requires that we consider alternative situations equally, and present both sides of a case for judgement. Economists are like advocates in law who could represent either the defence or the prosecution with equal, professional objectivity. Put two economists together, they say, and you will always hear four opinions.

Economics and Fashion

Where have those opinions taken economic thought over the years? There have been fashions and developments in economic thought as with so much else. One suggestion, put forward by Kondratieff, is of 'long waves' in economic and social life. These waves take perhaps fifty years or so to flow through and in so doing, they disturb many walks of life. Governments swing not just from free capitalism to directed socialism, but towards revolution and world war as well. Perhaps the same two-generation forces are reflected in social attitudes, of permissiveness or conventionality. Trends in economic thought would be a minor area for change by comparison.

Modern economics is usually traced back to the British Industrial Revolution, and in particular to Adam Smith's *Wealth of Nations* which was published in 1775. Microeconomic ideas such as division of labour and diminishing returns come from that time. By the 1840s, however, the concern was for more urgent policy and welfare questions. Comparative advantage and the justification for free trade, for free and perfect competition in general, sat squarely in the centre of the arguments of the day. One crucial argument was between the vested interests of landlords and the rising merchant classes over trade protection, and the Corn Laws to stop grain imports, in particular. Another was between the industrial entrepreneurs and the rising force of collective, unionised labour. The relevant areas of economic thought, on specialisation and exchange, against market dominance, are with us still today.

Microeconomics is based, at an introductory level at least, on a common approach. This adopts a mathematical treatment of costs and revenue for firms, satisfaction and spending for consumers, productivity and pay for workers. It uses also the marginalist approach mentioned above, looking at the effect of each extra unit or, more precisely, an infinitely small part of a unit. This identifies the direction of change and the precise nature of decision-making. But infinitely small changes are the clue to the pedigree of this theoretical approach. The theory of differential calculus was developed in mathematics in the latter part of the 1800s and adapted for use in a number of related disciplines, including economics. The marginalist approach was engrained in Marshall's *Principles of Economics* in 1890, and that exposition is still the basis for introductory courses of microeconomics today.

But economics is a modern science, we are told, developed mainly in the twentieth century. So what aspects of introductory economics have been thought out more recently? Macroeconomics has been the main area of development here, partly with the growth of government responsibility to control the performance of increasingly sophisticated national forces. But the analysis of growth, inflation, unemployment and international exchange makes great use also of traditional ideas. Classical economics, as it is now known, describes a world where national aggregates still reflect the market forces of microeconomics, and the behaviour of the whole economy is explained from its individual, component parts.

Keynesian economics, first expressed in Keynes's *General Theory of Employment, Interest and Money* in 1936, was a reaction against the apparent unrealism of that view. Imperfections and interrelationships could lead the macroeconomy into persistent imbalance as in the 1930s' slump. Direct government intervention through deficit financing was needed to control the economy from year to year, in this view and it held sway in government circles for the great growth period after the war. Disillusionment came because of escalating inflation and a return to slump, following the 1970s oil price crisis. But monetarism was not so much a new idea – Friedman's definitive article on the Quantity Theory of money and its significance for monetary discipline came in 1956 – as a return to traditional economic arguments. The new-classical and supply-side ideas of the 1970s and 1980s are a return to individual market forces, as well as a reaction against Keynesian orthodoxy. No doubt the next movement in economics will come as a reaction in turn against them. But will it involve something completely new to economic thought, or an adaptation of Keynesian ideas and approaches?

Must Economists Disagree?

Economics is a problem-solving subject. It asks questions arising from the central problem of scarcity and the implications for resource allocation. These questions never change very much from time to time. Even at macroeconomic level the questions continue to concentrate on national performance in terms of growth, jobs, inflation and international balance. But the answers seem to change significantly from one time to another. Economic theory has moved on from collective organisation, through the industrial age of free enterprise and market competition, then back again to Keynesian intervention and monetarist self-discipline. The complaint is not so much that there are too few answers to the questions of economics, as that there are too many!

The subject's controversies tend to repeat themselves, however, and to achieve a reconciliation of sorts. One long-running dispute is over the merits of free market forces against central control. Free enterprise allows the flexibility of individual motivation and initiative, so encouraging a speedy and accurate response to consumers' preferences. Central control directs resources according to a planned, overseen assessment of society's requirements. Both may be efficient, but in rather different senses. Free markets encourage cost-efficient production by firms and consumption by individuals but planning encourages overall allocation to reflect externalities for social efficiency. There are advantages and disadvantages to each. On balance, the mixed economies of the West prefer the freedom and cost efficiency of the market system but introduce government

action to correct and compensate for specific difficulties, such as
public goods or social costs.

Another argument continues at the macroeconomic level over
monetarist and Keynesian points of view. Much of this argument is
empirical, over the evidence in real world data for one or the other
point of view, rather than on analysis of theory. It tends to range
wider than over just the significance of changes in money supply
itself. Monetarism explains the role of money within its own market
area in terms of relative scarcity value. This classical, market view is
then extended by new classicists and supply-side economists to other
issues such as growth, the exchange rate and unemployment. But
market forces may take time to assert themselves in the macroeconomy while imperfections and misinformation abound. This allows
a reconciliation on timing at least with Keynesian economists.
Short-term demand management of spending through fiscal control
of public borrowing and monetary control of interest rates still plays
an important part in government policy. In pragmatic, policy terms
monetarist and Keynesian approaches seem reconciled on many
points, differing perhaps on questions of degree and the weight to be
allocated to different targets.

Certainly, there are differences between economists over the
causes and effects of economic behaviour, and people who expect
single and definite answers to their questions may find the subject
frustrating. Economics may offer different answers that each apply
to different conditions. Part of the appeal of the subject is that it
offers both sides of an argument the chance to be right, sometimes.
But it is based on people's behaviour in the real world, which cannot
be tested or controlled under precise laboratory conditions. The
economics lab is out in the shops, offices and factories of the world,
or more exactly, inside people's minds. Another part of its appeal is
in that everyday relevance and human interest.

It is as a social science that economics' search for objective,
permanent truth is doomed. Any answer economists reach about the
macroeconomy and how government might control it, for instance,
itself changes people's expectations and economic behaviour. Perhaps Keynesian economics was right in showing government how to
solve unemployment. But that led to new expectations that jobs
would be created, so unions acted more ruthlessly to raise pay and
the unemployed relied on government rather than themselves or

their labour market, to solve the problem. Thus inflation and unemployment returned, differently from before. It is the stimulation and variety of this constantly changing nature of the subject that gives it a further appeal: one never knows it all. Answering one question in economics only raises other and new questions. Our experience widens, but 'experience is the name everyone gives to their mistakes'.

Slipping the Chain

Fashions may come and go, controversies may swing in favour of one point of view or the other, but one theme is always present in economics. Close behind the questions of choice, of allocation and of macroeconomic performance comes the issue of 'what should be done about it?' High on the list of what gives economics its appeal sits its practical relevance and policy implications. Keynes said that he turned to economics because it seemed to combine the intellectual appeal of mathematics with the opportunity to do good. Few of us can know as much economics or do as much good as he, but we can share the same appeal. It is an opportunity that comes early in studying the subject.

Introductory courses in economics start with the basic skills of the economist, for data interpretation, understanding and expressing logical argument, and relating simple concepts to everyday situations. Basic economic principles include all the main areas of economic thought but concentrate on free market economics, marginalist microeconomics and Keynesian and monetarist macroeconomics. Advanced courses study more specialised areas such as industrial, labour market, or international economics. Related disciplines include statistics, economic history, politics and social development.

At all these different levels, however, questions of government policy arise. How can the government encourage competition and control monopoly? How can it achieve strong growth and balanced development by freeing, or constraining market forces? How can it control inflation without undue harm to unemployment? These and other questions arise naturally from the nature of economic material and method, but also from the interests of those studying the subject. The pedigree of the subject, as seen above, lies in the contemporary political and social issues of the day. The roots of modern economics lie in political economy as it was once, and is still practised.

But how does this equate with the demand for objective, value-free analysis as being the nature of positive economics and the training in every introductory course? Clearly, the two approaches are not the same. But it is the purpose of training that economists should identify for themselves, and inform others whom they advise, where objective and rational predictions stop and subjective opinions begin. It is one thing to predict how tax reforms will affect incentives, growth and the distribution of incomes, but it is another to say that those effects are preferable to others. It is the economist's role to predict how inflation may damage competitiveness and fixed income earners but it is the politician's to decide whether that damage is acceptable or not.

Of course, we all have something of the politician as well as the training of an economist within us all. Life would be very dull and disappointing if we had either one alone. The growth of economics as a subject is because of the light it throws on political, and management and financial and other decisions. In answering its own narrow questions about relationships, cause and effect economics opens up many other, wider questions altogether. It offers more questions, therefore, as well as answers. Among these we would find questions of judgement about the character found in this book and described above. Economic beings are self-motivated within the context of the economic model of free market behaviour. That motivation is rational, given the circumstances laid down for them by economic theory. Its conclusions about efficiency, resource allocation and performance of the economy are built on this narrow view of individuals' behaviour.

From outside and beyond positive economic theory, we can ask wider questions. Do we think our economic being is a realistic description of people's hopes and feelings? Do we accept that society must operate on the basis only of such individual, economic characteristics? The answer to both questions is surely – no. People show consideration and conscience even in a commercial arena, either as individuals or collectively through social, community and governmental groups. Is such behaviour economically irrational? – yes. Is it desirable? – that is a question that falls outside the confines of economics.

Index